Manna
in the
Morning

Manna in the Morning

A MEMOIR
1940–1958

Madeleine Stuart

Edited and introduced by Dermot Bolger

RAVEN ARTS PRESS / DUBLIN
COLIN SMYTHE / BUCKS.

This book is published by

THE RAVEN ARTS PRESS
P.O. Box 1430
Finglas
Dublin 11
Republic of Ireland

COLIN SMYTHE LTD.
P.O. Box 6
Gerrards Cross
Buckinghamshire
England

ISBN Raven 0 906897 81 5 (softback)
0 906897 82 3 (hardback)

Colin Smythe 0 86140 222 (softback)
0 86140 221 (hardback)

The Raven Arts Press would like to acknowledge that it receives financial assistance from the Arts Council *(An Chomhairle Ealaíon)*, Dublin, Ireland, for many of its publications.

Typesetting and make-up by Máire Davitt (Vermilion), Clondalkin, Dublin. Edited and designed by Dermot Bolger. Cover design and photographic design by Syd Bluett. Printing and binding by Confidential Report Printing, Dublin. Hardback binding by Tom Duffy, Duffy Bookbinding Ltd., Dublin.

Manna
in the
Morning

INTRODUCTION

Manna in the Morning tells the remarkable story of two journeys undertaken by a young Kashubian girl, in the company of one of the most original and finest Irish writers of this century. A physical journey from the streets of war-time Berlin through a slow flight across Europe, to Munich as it suffered its most severe bombing, on to refugeee camps and prison cells, intense hardship and near starvation in Dornbirn and Freiburg, and years of poverty in Paris and London, until, finally in 1958, they are able to settle into their first real home, a small cottage in the Co. Meath countryside of Ireland. But it is also the story of an inward journey and growth, of spiritual awakening through love and the poetry of Rilke and Keats and an intense personalised religious faith in the face of often seemingly impossible material obstacles. Yet one of the most astonishing features of the book is that despite many of the conditions and upsets they endured *Manna in the Morning* is a deeply joyous story, shot through with humour and the zeal for living and for the other great obsessions in this couple's life together, like horse racing and gambling, good wine and literature. Today *Black List, Section H* is becoming regarded as one of the most important Irish novels of the century, and in *Manna in the Morning* we have the unusual reversal of one of the central characters in such a major work actually retelling the events of the last part of *Black List* from her own viewpoint, alongside with the main events of *The Pillar of Cloud*, another of Stuart's major novels, which we can see from this book was based very closely on their experiences after the war in Freiburg. But above all these other considerations *Manna in the Morning* is first and foremost a love story of our times.

Madeleine (christened Gertrud) Meissner was born in Danzig, of Kashubian-Catholic parents on the 23rd of November, 1915, in the same hospital as another Kashubian, Günter Grass, was born twelve years later. Kashubia is that part of Poland south of Danzig (now more famous because of Lech Walesa and Solidarity as Gdansk) which was known after the first World War as "The Corridor", which separated the German Reich from East Prussia. Trains passing through it were not allowed to stop and their doors were locked. The Kashuben were an old ethnic tribe who had come from the Far East in a mass migration in early times, and unlike other ethnic tribes in Poland, had never risen in the social and economic scale. In fact they occupied roughly the same position as the Irish peasant, and similarly were the butt of much racial humour and bias. As the grandmother of Mr Grass's diminutive hero in *The Tin Drum* says, "The Kashubens are no good at moving. Their business is to stay where they are and hold out their heads for everyone else to hit, because we're not real Poles and we're not real Germans, and if you're a Kashube, you're not good enough for the Germans or the Polacks. They want everything full measure." As well illustrated in *The Tin Drum,* the Kashubes were forced in the years leading up to the second World War to choose between the two nationalities, and this led to a major split in the Meissner family, with Madeleine's father choosing the German side, while most of his relations chose to identify with Poland — a decision for which they were almost all liquidated by Hitler in 1939.

Just after the end of the Great War in 1919, Madeleine's family fled from Poland and settled in the small town of Lauban where her father taught until his death from consumption in 1921. Her mother was left to raise the family of four girls (of which Madeleine was the second youngest) on a small pension and they remained there in relatively severe poverty in a small flat until 1929 when Frau Meissner grew homesick for her family. As they were unable to return to Poland they settled in Danzig-Olivia, a suburb of Danzig until 1936 when they moved to Berlin where the girls were more likely to find employment. After finishing school Madeleine's main desire in life was to study in Berlin university, which in those days of restricted travel represented freedom and the unravelling of new worlds for her. This desire led her into conflict with her mother who had clearly defined plans for her to become a national schoolteacher. After leaving school Madeleine completed a one year secretarial course in the Lette-Haus in Berlin and worked in a number of temporary office jobs and for a brief period in a bank. This was one of the most unhappy periods of her life and finally she gave in to her mother's request and enroled in a training school for national teachers. Before she could begin her studies she had to complete a statutory six months in a labour camp working on the land that all young Germans wishing to study had to attend. However she left the training school after only a few weeks and went to her eldest sister in former Poland, near the Russian border until her mother sent her a telegram telling her that she could come home and enter university. In January 1940 she began her studies in Berlin university where soon after she met and fell in love with Francis Stuart.

The path of Francis Stuart to become a lecturer in Berlin is slightly more complex, and while it is well known to readers of his work, I will mention it briefly here as I feel *Manna in the Morning* may be of interest to a broader readership. Francis Stuart was born in Australia in 1902, of Northern Irish Protestant stock. Four months after his birth Stuart's father died in undisclosed circumstances in a mental home in Townsville, and his mother returned to Ireland with him. He attended various schools in Dublin and England, including Rugby, where in 1916 he heard word of the Easter Rising. In 1920, at the age of eighteen, he met Iseult Gonne, (the natural daughter of Maud Gonne and a noted French politician, Lucien Millevoye), who was slightly older that Stuart and considerably more experienced, having been proposed to by Yeats, and briefly been the mistress of Ezra Pound. They fled to London where they lived together for four months before returning to Dublin where they were married and lived under the watchful eyes of Iseult's mother. In 1922 Stuart participated in the Irish Civil War on the Republican side, and was imprisoned in Portlaoise and Tintown for just under a year. Shortly after his release in November 1923 he issued his first book, a collection of poems entitled *We Have Kept the Faith*. In 1929 he moved with Iseult to Laragh in Co. Wicklow and two years later his first novel was published.

Initially Francis Stuart enjoyed an almost dazzling success as a novelist, with his two 1932 novels, *Pigeon Irish* and *The Coloured Dome* receiving major critical acclaim. Yeats wrote of *Pigeon Irish,* "This has the same cold, exciting strangeness, attained less by beautiful passages, though there are such passages in plenty, than by construction, characterisation and a single dominating aim." But from the early highpoint of these two books his literary output began to decline in quality, although his books still remained relatively popular. Basically Stuart was existing under the sort of economic pressure that required him to release over one book a year, with little opportunity for revision or radical new artistic concepts. In total in the 1930s he produced eleven novels, one volume of autobiography and a book entitled *Racing for profit and pleasure in Ireland and elsewhere,* which was to serve as a bible for many connoisseurs of the turf.

Needless to say there were a number of factors in addition to his declining career which prompted Stuart to accept the invitation in 1939 to travel to Berlin as a citizen of a neutral country to lecture there in literature. On a family level Stuart seems to have married Iseult with his vision of her clouded by her romantic position in the poetry of Yeats. Although they remained together, on no level could the marriage have really been described as a success. Like many people who marry too young they simply grew up and apart. By the thirties they were bound together in a web of mutual hostility, antipathy and inability to communicate. In these circumstances Europe presented a means of escape where he could be confident he would be stranded for a number of years.

However, we come closer to discovering the real reasons when we examine his repeated and deliberate alienation of himself from the easy options of society around him as if it were only possible to breathe freely when cast out from the secure strictures of accepted thoughts and actions. In his early teens Stuart wrote a letter in support of home rule to a Dublin newspaper on his Unionist relations headed notepaper. The impulse to do so came not from any great political conviction, but from an instinct, not fully understood for years, to cut himself off from the moral and social integrity of his family. This obsession with being an outsider possibly goes back to a kinship with the father he never knew, and was to be the centrepoint of Stuart's work and life in the coming years. In his work his main characters similarly have to commit acts of defiance against the conventional morality of the society they exist in before they can start to function as the inner beings they are. At the end of *The Coloured Dome* the hero, after being given a chance to give his life in exchange for that of a number of political prisoners and then having the offer taken from him, is unable to adjust back to his normal mundane role in life, and prefers to have himself thrown back in jail, this time in a squalid cell among the usual drunks and petty thieves picked up during the night. "Now utterly stripped and humbled, the cold snows poured through Garry Delea's heart and he waited in this silence without impatience, sitting straight on the narrow bench. And while he waited he humbly offered himself, in that cold and peaceful holocust to share the little, ludicrous tragedies of the world." These strange fictional lines echo in sentiment the final autobiographical lines of *Black List* over thirty years later as if by his actions Stuart had deliberately turned the ideas of his fiction into reality. "The cell, on his return, appeared dim and shabby to the point of being uninhabitable, and it was hard to see how he had ever looked on it, or his own corner of its floor, as a tolerable shelter. But soon he was reconciled to it again. Although he was still far from coming to understand the necessity of what had happened to them, he did begin to see the silence that he had entered as the deep divide between the past and what was to come. Whatever it was that was at the other end there was no way of telling. It might be a howl of final despair or the profound silence might be broken by words that he didn't yet know how to listen for."

Another clue to Stuart's later behaviour is found in his 1935 book *The Angel of Pity*, which begins, "I imagine a grey morning breaking over some desolate front in the next great war. I am crouching in a concrete redoubt, partially blown-in, with one companion, the sole survivors of a waste of mud and water reflecting the concrete-coloured sky." Francis Stuart was deeply committed to De Valera's policy of neutrality in the case of a coming war, but if there was to be such a war then he was determined to be a part of it, not as a combatant on either side, but as "the last unsilenced voice, the only one left to make a gesture of defiance." There is a perceptive line in Patrick

10

Kavanagh's *Lough Derg*, written in 1942, when he says, "All Ireland that froze for want of Europe." Clearly it would be impossible to remain in Ireland and yet to be involved, to record the destruction of one world, and possibly help to create the ideas from which another world might rise from the ruins.

As Robert Fisk remarks in his book, *The Time of War*, Stuart was not a fascist, "but he felt a powerful attraction towards the new order that was preparing to overthrow the old capitalist order." Politically Stuart was as immature as he was emotionally at the time of his marriage. As he says in *Black List*, "Lord Haw Haw's polemics left H cold. It wasn't the political or military events that concerned him but the possible inner revolution that he hoped the war might bring about." Before arriving in Germany Stuart had the idea of Hitler as "a super dissident", not realising that the German leader had, in fact, the very sort of bourgeois, middle-class shopkeeper mentality that Stuart was running from. "(he) had an old woman's sucked-in mouth and a way of clasping his hands in front of him as if he wished to tuck them under an apron." Far from being in any way committed to the German Reich Stuart began to contemplate a visit to Russia as disillusionment set in and his hopes turned towards Stalin. "Stalin struck H as a monster in the Dostoevskyan tradition. If Hitler was a mongrel dog barking and snarling at closed doors — had they been opened to him he'd have crawled in wagging his tail — Stalin was silent, solitary, contemtuous both of his enemies and allies."

However, even in this state of disillusionment Stuart was to make another decision which was to firmly close the door on his former life, his literary reputation and, for a time after the war, his personal liberty, by deciding to do a series of broadcasts to Ireland. "Being in Germany was one thing, lecturing at Berlin university was bad enough — but . . . I had the opportunity of doing something that would cut me off from all the *bien pensants* in society . . . That was the one aim I did have. I think I did have some idea of a new Europe in which Ireland would be involved although I didn't know how this would happen. I was very confused." In contrast to the talks of William Joyce and Hartmann, Stuart's broadcasts to Ireland must have baffled most of his listeners. He began his talks with the words, "I am not trying to make propaganda,"and over the following months expanded his views on Ireland's role in a new imaginary Europe, ("our own life on our own soil, free from the tyranny of money"), mixed with statements of support for Ireland's neutrality and discussions on Irish poetry and literature, including the work of P.H. Pearse and a play on St Patrick's night which he wrote about the blind poet Raftery. These broadcasts, it must be said, really pleased nobody, including the German authorities who constantly applied more presssure on him to place greater political emphasis on his talks, until he finally found it impossible to continue broadcasting. While certainly by no means as innocent as, for example, the talks for which P.G. Wodehouse was later ostracised in Britain, the actual effect of these broadcasts to Ireland by Stuart appear to have been almost nil. While almost everybody remembered the voice of Lord Haw Haw, who was afforded an almost cult-hero notority in parts of the countryside, Stuart was to find on his return to Ireland that "I hardly ever met anybody who heard me. I don't think anybody really listened." However, the personal effects of these broadcasts were to totally transform his life and future career. Working in the almost impossible conditions he had created for himself in their wake he was to turn his experiences of rejection and imprisonment into two of his greatest novels immediately after the war, and to go on producing novels throughout the fifties, until his second long silence in the sixties and then the late harvest of major works, starting with *Black List,* and continuing with *Memorial,* which is being re-issued by Raven to coincide with this book, *A Hole in the Head, The High Consistory,* and a new novel, *Faillandia,* just completed at the age of eighty two.

However I feel it would be wrong to attribute the new maturity and strength of Stuart's post war books to his experiences in the war alone. I think that Stuart is one of those people for whom security and stability can not be considered in terms of physical comfort or even having a roof over one's head, but in terms of a secure lasting relationship. Perhaps for the first time with Madeleine, Francis Stuart had such security to rely on and be able to draw strength from. And visiting them today one senses in their home that small commune of peace that the characters of many of his novels

12

struggled to establish.

Madeleine Stuart is one of the most colourful and interesting conversationalists I have had the pleasure of knowing. However, like many people to whom English is a second language her flow of language does not always conform to the strictures of English grammar. In editing this book I have striven to find a happy medium between retaining the character and excitement of her original typescript and making the language as accessible as possible to general readers.

To just complete the story Francis and Madeleine Stuart lived in their small cottage, with Francis' mother for the brief period before her death, until the early seventies, when they moved to a small house in Windy Arbour in Dublin where they now live. The years that followed were still full of difficulties for Stuart's career; his major novel *Black List, Section H* was rejected by many publishers, his play *Who Fears to Speak* commissioned by the Abbey Theatre was stopped late in rehearsals because of its content, and when he finally found a new publisher in Timothy O'Keeffe of Martin, Brian & O'Keeffe, his 1972 novel *Memorial* was held up in the Irish customs and he was denied access to copies of it for several months. Madeleine found work teaching and typing in Meath and when they moved to Dublin started work in St Kilian's German school in the city. Just after Francis' eightieth birthday and thanks to *Aosdána*, Madeleine, for the first time in her life, was finally able to stop working. As I have said earlier, above all these other considerations, *Manna in the Morning* is first and foremost a love story. And I am pleased to say that it is one which continues unabashed and even stronger today.

Dermot Bolger,
Finglas,
October, 1984.

Madeleine Stuart outside Berlin
University, 1941

Madeleine and Francis Stuart,
Berlin, 1941

Madeleine and her sister, Traute,
Berlin Park, 1941

PROLOGUE

I remember the days of old;
I meditate on all Thy work
I muse on the work of Thy hands. (143)

She stood mesmerised before the booth at the fairground, as if
her feet were unable to move. All her being was concentrated
on that magical rainbow-coloured ball on the shelf. She should
have been home by now, as it was already dark, but was
too absorbed in the game going on before her. If you bought a
ticket you had a chance to win all kinds of toys and sweets, and
if you were especially lucky, the main prize — the big ball. But
she had no money left, as the ten Pfennig that her mother had
given her had been long spent on a ride on the white elephant
on the merry-go-round. She loved the image of him appearing
every few seconds among the other animsls, *"und dann und
wann ein weisser Elephant."* (And now and then a white
elephant — Rilke.) She knew that each night towards the end
the proprieter of the booth always gave away some tickets
free, and now, at last, after a long patient wait she was the
holder of one of these tickets. The wheel kept spinning round
and one prize after the other went, until the tension rose as the
big prize came, and the wheel stood still on number 27. But
nobody shouted "here". The man called again "No 27 for the
magic ball!' The little girl was so intense that she didn't look
at her ticket until somebody nudged her and said, "Hey, you
have it." He called out for her and this time the proprietor was
delighted to hand over the prize to a child. "But you should be
in bed, you know," he said to her, and she nodded and with the
precious gift against her breast she hurried through the fair-

ground, with just one quick glimpse of the white elephant doing its rounds. And her mother forgave her, of course, when she saw the happiness of her little girl. She would keep the ball safe in a niche in her play-corner, and not expose it to rough games in the street. Anyhow it would not bounce like a tennis ball, it was different. Only from time to time would she have a secret game with it, throwing it up into the air and catching it as it flew back to her like a multi-coloured bird.

Chapter One

BERLIN 1940

January of 1940 was bitterly cold, with ice and snow everywhere. The university term had already begun, but Mr Stuart, the new lecturer from Ireland, hadn't arrived yet, having probably been delayed by the war. But finally one day in mid-January he appeared and gave his first lecture to us students.

My first impression of him was of a tall lanky figure in grey flannel trousers and a dark-blue pullover, of the kind fishermen wear, with one hand in his pocket and the other swinging by his side. He walked loose-limbed, as I imagined a sailor would on firm ground after a long sea voyage, and had a good mop of brown-greyish hair, a remarkable bony face with good jaws, a large forehead, deep-set grey-blue eyes with heavy eye-lids, a broad mouth and a most engaging, gentle smile.

My second impression of him was of astonishment and relief that somebody teaching in a university should come in so casually dressed. All our professors dressed in dark well-pressed suits with white collars and cufflinks. It was a pleasure that somebody could come in, completely different, who seemed to bring with him another way of life. I had never before seen anything like it. Everything about him seemed to me to be wonderful, the way in which he walked, dressed and talked with such freedom. I caught a glimpse of another world that would gradually become clear to me. Looking back I am surprised at the instinct I had then, which has never left me, and has been my guiding star in life.

Some of my fellow students would purse their lips at his completely non-academic manner of lecturing, which again struck me as being totally different from anything I had previously heard or seen, and which I liked. We were informed that

Mr Stuart was a writer, but this meant nothing to me. I could not imagine a living writer. This was because we were brought up on the old masters and the classics, but were rarely given a glimpse of a modern writer. The modern ones, apparently, had to die before they were included in any curriculum. But whether I grasped that he was a writer or not, it didn't take anything away from the way in which he introduced us to Irish poets and writers, books and poems.

No one had ever spoken to us as he did, opening up a new mysterious world. He read out poems or passages from novels in a peculiar uniform, undramatic, and yet sad and haunting way. Gradually Ireland became alive for me, that little island which I knew vaguely from geography lessons, with its ruins and history, its songs of lament and homesickness, and its sad love and struggle for freedom.

I am haunted by numberless islands, and many
* a Danaan shore*
Where time would surely forget us, and sorrow
* come near us no more,*
Soon far from the rose and the lily, and fret of
* the flames would we fly,*
Were we only white birds, my beloved, bouyed out on
* the foam of the sea!*

(The White Birds by Yeats)

So the first Trimester went by (because of the war the academic year was no longer divided into two semesters, but three. This was meant to hasten up the years of study), and then the second. We were already in the third winter Trimester.

Amongst our English conversation classes with Mr Stuart there was a kind elderly lady who invited all eight of us students to a little *Adventsfeier* on the first Advent-Sunday at her home, which was not far from where I lived. We all went, laughing and giggling, lit the first candle on the wreath, then sang some Advent songs and afterwards had *Pfefferkuchen.* While we were celebrating Mr Stuart came, apologised with a smile for being a little late, and joined in the celebrations. He was unable to stay long, and before leaving had a few words in the hall with our hostess. He had asked her if any of the students

18

might be able to do some typing for him. This immediately interested me. I had no fees to pay then, because children in a family of four or more in Germany at that time who had a good standard of intelligence were given free university education. However I had to bring some income in to help my mother, who was a widow, to run the household. So I had taken up a number of typing jobs in offices in my spare time.

The moment I got home I went to the telephone booth opposite our house and phoned Mr Stuart to inquire about the kind of job he had in mind, and if I might apply for it. And that banal little telephone conversation proved to be the turning point of my life. Happy as a lark I skipped across the snowy street home. But it was not only to me that something had happened, something had also happened to Mr Stuart when he realised who I was. As he later told me, he had noticed me in his small essay and conversation classes for my interest and participation which, he felt, made the whole thing a bit lively.

Many years later, in *Black List, Section H,* Francis was to remember that telephone conversation:

> 'He was trying to put a face to the unexpected voice out of the receiver . . . H. stood in the big room with the black-out blinds over the three windows and only the table lamp lit . . . hearing the low, foreignly accented words echo out of the ebony shell. There were a handful of brassy Pfennige, mark and two-mark pieces with a dim silver sheen in a china bowl, and these he saw not as usual submerged in the present flowing over them, but suddenly exposed and made unique by a shift in the tide of time.'

We met the next afternoon at the corner of Charlottenstrasse Unter den Linden and went together to the *Drahtlose Dienst* (radio station) where Mr Stuart translated some of the German news into English. As his previous secretary had left I was taken on there and then. The work consisted of a few hours in the late afternoon and so did not interfere with my studies in the university. Naturally I had to do the preparations for the next day's lectures or seminars at night. I was often exhausted and to remain awake would put my feet in a bucket of cold water and drink strong black coffee and remain up until well after midnight.

If ever there was such a thing as fate in life, then that was it. After a completely unadventurous and restricted home life the floodgates seemed to have opened for me. Now everything had taken on a different, radiant look. The hours spent in that small cubby hole of an office were a haven to me, the dark wintery afternoons became aglow. Something had struck me like lightning (whether I knew at that time what it really was does not matter), that was never to be eradicated from my life. For better or worse I had found my vocation.

Whenever there was a lull in the translation and typing work we went down to the *Kneipe* (pub) on the ground floor of the *Drahtlose Dienst*. There we would take some wine and talk, Mr Stuart about Ireland, especially his home, Laragh, and the lakes of Glendalough, and I about my undistinguished, lovable homeland of the *Kaschubei*, South of Danzig. The Kaschuben were an old ethnic tribe who migrated from the Far East in early times and settled in that part of Poland now known as Kashubia. Rather like the Irish farmers at the start of the century they existed mainly on potatoes which they grew in poor sandy soil. Much of the land was covered with bog and they were the butt of jokes from many prosperous Poles. It was only later in life when I read Günther Grass' novel, *The Tin Drum*, that I really became proud of my background. His background was the same as mine and he was even born in the same hospital of Danzig-Langfuhr as I was.

If we remained in the office and had some time to spare we would look at art cards and through them I was introduced to artists like Van Gogh, Gaugin and others. Or else he would tell me about writers and their work, such as the Brontes, Hemingway who was then very much in fashion, Dostoyevsky and others. There seemed no end to that miraculous world. It was a world of the imagination that I had only been vaguely aware of. Outside that office it was dark and cold and frosty, but within there burnt a strange fire.

On New Year's Eve, 1940, we went out for the first time to a restaurant, the *Nikolsburger Krug,* close to the Pension Naumann on Nikolsburger Platz where Mr Stuart lived. After a meal with red wine, when he saw me home (I lived just around the corner) he hugged me for the first time. And I think that from that evening he became Francis.

On the 20th of March, 1941, Francis went on a holiday to Munich as the university had a short break. I was worried that he might never come back to that little office which had held so much magic for us, but he said, and I wrote down in my diary that night: "It would be funny if I did not return to this office. I have no need to go to the university. I would not miss it. But with you in this office it is another thing. It is part of my life. I was very unhappy coming into the office, but when seeing you there . . . " So these words had to console me while he was away. When he came back to the office after the holiday we still had that friend-relationship between us, which was fine for a while. But gradually I realised that it was not enough for me. I seemed to go up in flames, while Francis remained calm and detached. Being near him and yet not being able to be tender to each other I found very painful and outside the office I became wretched and cried myself to sleep at night. So in the middle of May that year I came to the conclusion that it was better to finish working there and to end our friendship. I knew that Francis liked me all right, but I did not feel he cared enough. I was not aware at the time that he could not enter into a proper relationship with me until he was through with another one in Berlin. That relationship had finished but he was still not yet free from it.

So I told him of my dilemma, but he had nothing to say to comfort me. And now my heart was desolate. I thought things over for the next few days and on Sunday (we sometimes had to work Sundays as well because of the news) I told him that I was quitting the place. It would not be very difficult to find another job. He was aghast when he realised that I was serious about it and, without arguing, simply took me in his arms and hugged me saying: "Please stay on, I need you." I would have liked to hear something more, but I was content with this. He seemed miserable and I realised how little I knew about his worries and determined that if I could brighten up his life a little, then I would.

Soon we went out to celebrate our new union to the *Troika,* near Tauentzinplatz, a nice Russian restaurant, where as we dined, Francis suddenly came out with, "I love you." God Almighty — that flash went right to my heart and I can still remember the date, May 28th, 1941.

When the summer holidays came around again Francis wanted to go to Vienna on July 14th. On the day before his departure we said good-bye properly over a bottle of red wine and there and then he hugged and kissed me as never before. That summer was long and hot, but there were no special signs of war in Berlin except for ration cards. Life continued as usual. I went on working in the office, sometimes for the English and sometimes the Irish *Redaktion* (radio). At home I tried to work hard at my studies, but my heart was no longer there, it was somewhere else.

Then Francis wrote asking me to join him for the rest of his holidays in Vienna, and as much as I would have liked to go, I could not. My mother, as yet, didn't know anything of our relationship, except that we both worked in the Rundfunkhaus (Broadcasting House). The Irish and English Redaktion had moved to the huge Rundfunk building at the end of the Ost-West-Achse, in the Masurenallee. So Francis returned home to Berlin much earlier. I remember so well that glorious sunny day, September the 18th, when we finally met again at the corner of Kaiserallee-Hohenzollerndamm and took the U-Bahn (metro) to the Grunewald, one of a number of beautiful old forests around Berlin. We picniced there each afternoon for the next few days. It was a heavenly time for both of us.

On the 27th of September I went with Francis to his room in the pension at the corner of Kurfürstendamm-Uhlandstrasse. While we were sitting together at the open window in the dusk, a bottle of white wine was cooling under the dripping water tap in the sink. We sipped the wine, drew the curtain and then, as had to happen, we became lovers. A few days later I went to visit my aunt near Danzig and Francis sent me the following poem in one of a number of his letters which were waiting for me when I reached there.

I am poor as the hawk is poor
With naught but a blunted wing
Stretched over depths of air
And cannot sing!
We can only bleed or make bleed,
Or should I say: love or die
Must those of that desolate breed —
The hawk and I?

At Halloween Francis gave a small party in his new room in Rankestrasse. There were two Russian friends, Herr Jensch, a student girl and myself. We played some records, danced to the music and drank red wine, which was not difficult to get in those days.

Francis had given up his job as translator when he returned from Vienna. But he still gave talks to Ireland from the Irish Redaktion. Dr Hartmann was over the department and he would broadcast news in Irish to Ireland, which must have had a tiny audience.

On Christmas Eve Francis came to my home. We celebrated Holy Eve with the traditional goose which, strictly speaking, is served on Christmas day in Germany. On Holy Eve something like fish or a salad is usually served. My mother liked Francis very much and so far did no suspect anything between us, although Francis had given me a little ring with a green stone a few days before. I lied to mother about the ring, which I was so happy to wear on my finger, and said, of all things, that Mr Joyce, who also worked in the English department and for whom I had often typed and had shared many a bottle of wine with in the nearby *Lokal*, had given me the ring out of pure friendship. I liked William Joyce, who was known in England as Lord Haw-Haw, as a person. An Irishman, he was always in high spirits, bristled with energy and brought a whiff of life into the office where he was popular with everybody. Much later I saw what a courageous man he was. When one night there was a heavy bomber attack everybody fled to the *Luftschutzkeller*. But he had remained in the office, gone to the window and looked out at the sky with the bombs falling in the distance. I stayed with him, after he had assured me that the bombers did not, as yet, drop their bombs over residential districts, but concentrated on the industrial surroundings of Berlin. I knew little of politics at that time. My father had died early and my mother was too engrossed in attempting to raise her four children to pay much attention to anything outside her own home. But that night, standing at the dark window, gazing out at the bombs, I was impressed by him and was glad to have shared those few moments with him.

Much later, in the aftermath of the war, when I was arrested by the French together with Francis and thoroughly searched, they found a newspaper cutting about the arrest of Mr Joyce (who was executed by the British for his broadcasts) in my handbag. This increased their suspicion that I was a dangerous person and possibly, along with Francis, a spy.

Around that time in Berlin Francis wrote a number of poems for me. This one was written on December the 28th, 1941.

I had no peace when there was peace,
I had no light when all was lit
By the world's glittering wealth and ease.
I saw a noisy swarm of bees
Around an empty hive of death.
But now within the bloody pit
of war, the wound, the chained desire,
The ache within my every breath
That burnt my life up with its fire,
And was so mocked by the world's peace,
Has found in you at last release.

When Francis gave up his job in the English Redaktion after the Summer holidays of 1941 that world of our own which we had created came to an end. But a new arrangement was quickly found. I would go to his cosy little room in Rankestrasse as soon as possible after university, as I now worked night-shift in the *Redaktion.* It was usually dusk when I arrived. In one corner he had an electric cooker, cups and saucers, even a pot to make some stew and often he would make real coffee. This was a great luxury and was only available on the black market. Normally we would drink Ersatzkaffee. I would tell him about the different English lectures I had heard that day. This was all new and interesting, yet it would not have made an abiding impression on me if Francis hadn't conjured poets like Keats, Blake, Wordsworth and Shakespeare into real life figures. He would read out the poems and then reveal them in a new light which has remained with me up to the present day.

At that time and later on during the war Keats occupied us a lot. Many of his poems had the power to comfort us in the midst of a war that seemd to have no end. We believed in him as the prophet for a better world.

And other spirits there are standing apart
Upon the forehead of the age to come;
These, these will give the world another heart
And other pulses . . .   (Sonnet XIV)

Another of Keats' poems which meant a lot to us then was the second sonnet "On Fame" beginning:

How fevered is the man, who cannot look
Upon his mortal days with temperate blood
Who vexes all the leaves of his life's book,

In a world so full of violence and chaos Keats created for us a world of peace where we found hope and refuge. His universe was so rich and vast, he would create things which we enjoyed at that moment, when they were a pure luxury to us, but much later in life they were to become of great concern to us, like, for example, the world of animals. This is from "Endymion".

. . . Four maned lions hale
The sluggish wheels; solemn, their toothed maws,
Their surly eyes brow-hidden, heavy paws
Uplifted drowsily, and nervy tails
Covering their tawny brushes . . .

Forty years later Francis was to write a passage in *The High Consistory* describing a similar painting of a chariot drawn through an attic grove by a wild beast:

Transform her in the myth: that was the way to express what I knew about her. Paint her as a wood nymph, or local deity, garlanded with withered wild flowers from a bacchanalia. Let her recline half-naked in a chariot drawn by a camelopard.

Keats poured out all his emotion when he wrote to Fanny:

No, my sweet Fanny, I am wrong; I do not wish you to be unhappy — and yet I do, I must while there is so sweet a beauty — my lovliest — my darling! Good-bye! I kiss you. Oh the torment.

25

And three months before his death on February the 23rd, 1821, he wrote to Mrs Browne and added at the end a postscript meant for Fanny, with his last dying words to her: "Goodbye, Fanny. God bless you!" However the words to Fanny Browne that have always meant the most to me are: "Love is my religion." Gradually in these hours of reading alone in Francis' small flat we came to build up a "Jerusalem" of our own. This Jerusalem was not dependent on any "green and pleasant land." We brought it with us wherever we were, mainly through suffering, be it air-raids, flight, prison, mansarde (garret), or much later, a small cottage in Ireland. What an instinct we had to build it then because in later times we were to be in dire need of it.

If I forget you, o Jerusalem,
Let my right hand wither away;
Let my tongue cling to the roof of my mouth
If I do not remember you,
If I do not set Jerusalem
Above my highest joy.   (Psalm 137)

During the next summer of 1942 we stayed for eight weeks in the flat of Frau Weiland, who had translated Maud Gonne's book. "Servant of the Queen" into German near the *Reichssportfeld*. It was lovely to be finally able to share with Francis all the sweet moments of daily life, making breakfast, cooking, or just sitting on the balcony in the evening. Yet such happiness was often wrought with quarrels. I was (and still am) a highly volatile person. Yet this too was all a part of our progress.

Frank Ryan, who lived under an assumed name in Berlin, came to visit us with my younger sister Gretel, who was training to become a nurse. Frank and herself struck up a friendship, but it was not really serious on either side. Frank was highly romantic and his chivalry naturally impressed my sister. He spoiled her with presents and even went so far as to come home for lunch with my mother with whom he would have had little in common and whom he was slightly cautious of. I liked Frank who was an extraordinary generous man. He would take us out to the best restaurants, like the *Presseklub*, or *Stöckler am Kurfürstendamm*, and give Francis ration cards, as he had

Francis Stuart, passport photo, mid 1930s

Frank Ryan, 1930s

Francis and Madeleine in Berlin 1941

more than us, having diplomatic status. Himself and Francis loved to talk about politics, Ireland and the I.R.A., all subjects that Gretel and I had little interest in. But when Gretel finished her training as a nurse and got a job in Hamburg's Eppendorf Hospital, he used to visit her there. Sometimes we saw him in the evenings at his flat which he shared with Helmut Clissmann near the *Stadtpark*. Those parties were lively and there was no shortage of good food and drink. Helmut Clissmann struck me then, and still does today, as the ideal diplomat, always courteous, well-balanced, helpful and polite. It was a strange coincidence that when much later in life I found a job in the German school, St Kilian's in Ireland, and needed a reference that the then head of the Council was Helmut. Frank Ryan was amazingly neat and proper and I remember once finding him ironing his trousers. I imagine that this goes back to the discipline of a soldier's life in the I.R.A. in Ireland and the International Brigade in Spain. Frank was a bit deaf and I think this must have contributed to his occasional touchiness.

After we left Frau Weiland's flat we went for ten days to Vienna. This was a heavenly, peaceful time for both of us. I wrote in my diary: "No books, no work, no women interfered." So we must have suffered from them in Frau Weiland's flat. We were fascinated in the gallery by a picture, "Allegorie der Vergänglichkeit", (roughly: The passing of all time) by Pereda, representing a mysterious angel with dark outstretched wings. We seemed to find shelter under them.

But there was so much to absorb there: the old-fashioned trams, the cafés, wine-cellers, cobbled streets, and our old-fashioned hotel, *König von Ungarn*. We usually joined the people who after work went into the wine-cellers for a *Viertel* (quarter litre) or an *Achtel* (eighth of a litre) of wine, which was still easy to come by, unlike in Berlin. I loved the cellers which just had white-washed walls, deal tables with benches and barrels of wine.

We took a little tram to the races in Freudenau near Vienna. It was an old-fashioned, intimate and slightly dilapidated racecourse, which could have done with a coat of paint. There I plunged for the favourite, *Gestiefelte Kater,* in a three horse race only to see him beaten. And I took it so much to heart that I cried over it. But Francis had words of comfort, although they were a bit puzzling I must say, "That's racing, my love," and a glass of wine soon helped me over the hurdle. But I have never forgotten the incident and in a three horse race I always go for the outsider.

We took a trip to Baden-Baden, where we sat on a grass slope overlooking a small village surrounded by mountains. It was difficult to believe that there was a war raging — here you could breathe and touch the peace. It was in such contrast to the sinister hell of the gambling Casino which we walked through later that evening.

A very religious experience for us was the visit to Beethoven's house, where we actually touched the piano and took in the view from his window where he sat and composed music, deaf to the sound of the world.

Yes, in that bare room
than mountains higher,
above the world and the tomb
there was light, there was fire.
The boards which we trod
where truth, where God
had burnt into a soul.
What desire, what unrest
to have stood there and known
the still warm, empty nest
whence the phoenix had flown.

(Francis, Sept., 23rd, 1942)

And finally there was the memorable, last evening in the *Stephansdom,* where a *Bachkonzert* was given. There we sat in the dusk with those beautifully painted windows glowing in the last rays of a setting sun. The organ and the other instruments took us into a world of bliss that we had never experienced through music before.

Mother would have strongly objected to my going with Francis, but luckily for my sister and her boyfriend and Francis and myself she had left us by this stage and gone to live with her eldest daughter who was married in what was formerly Poland. She had become disgruntled with us, felt out of place and naturally, being a very strict, narrow-minded Catholic, did not approve of our carrying on. But I have to ask myself was it really the Church which had struck terror into her for the

29

safety of our souls?

In my case I feel there was a deeper root to it. Mother had envisaged a life with me teaching and her keeping the household for me. I seemed to remind her so much of her dead husband in bearing and spirit that I was meant to fill that gap of lost love within her. I was "her one and all" as she once told me. She had given in to Francis and myself in so far as to accept our relationship for the duration of the war. She would say to me: "Be happy as long as the war lasts, then Mr Stuart will go back to Ireland," meaning that mother and I would then live together for the rest of our lives. That thought deeply depressed me. Francis and I at that time never contemplated the future, we didn't have to as there was an implicit understanding that nothing would part us. It was a pity that mother was so stubborn and unyielding, not only in regards to Francis, but to life in general. She would sooner put her head through a wall than try and adapt herself to a new situation. So she died a very lonely and embittered person in Poland, where neither of us could visit the other because of the frontiers between us. The last time I saw her was with my older sister in September 1942.

And so I had my birthday in November without her for the first time. I missed her very much, as she had the gift of making our simple home and our feasts into a warm, loving celebration.

With the new year of 1943 everything became worse. The air-attacks at night were regular and heavier, the food situation became more desparate, and, on top of that, a Siberian-like winter had set in. Perhaps that winter may have only felt colder, as we had little heat and almost no nourishing food. It snowed in huge white drifts which were not cleared away, but just piled up on the edge of the pavements. Children loved it as they could play hide-and-seek there. Everywhere heating became a major problem. We sat through lectures in our boots and coats with gloves on. At this time the thoughts of the *Staatsexamen* (final exam) which seemed to loom over me, terrified me. I had to work so hard for it that I was forced to give up my night job at the Redaktion. Anyway there seemed to be little point in earning money, as you couldn't buy anything with it, except at very high prices on the black market. I wrote in my diary: "I am so afraid of the examination, I am so stupid and forget everything. My mind is a sieve, I only wish that I could love Francis from morning to night instead of all this studying." The words of Keats to Fanny Browne, "Love is my religion" still haunted me, and I felt them become more and more real to me, until they became a kind of gospel.

To try and get some respite from this outward misery we went from April the 8th to the 20th to the *Tippelbaude* in the *Riesengebirge.* Here the peace was simply wonderful, there were no alarms and the war seemed far away. We went with a toboggan for walks in the snow-covered forests, which were breathtakingly beautiful. After lunch we usually sun-bathed. Once we climbed the Schneekoppe, the highest mountain in this part of the world, on top of which stood a chapel to the Blessed Virgin. A cold wind seemed to blow there, day and night. The Schneekoppe dominated not only the landscape, but also the lives of the people. If the mountain was not visible first thing in the morning it normally meant a long period of snow. And on one day we were there a blizzard raged all day and nobody could venture outdoors. But there was plenty of wood and we remained warm and cosy. The blizzard gave us a chance to read some of the books we had brought with us together, one of which was "The Revelations of Divine Love of Juliana of Norwich". We both especially love the passage in it about the hazel nut:

Also HE shewed a little thing, the size of a hazel-nut, which seemed to lie in the palm of my hand, and it was as round as any ball . . . 'What may this be?' I was answered in a general way, thus: 'It is all that is made' . . . I wondered how long it could last . . . And I was answered . . . 'It lasts, and ever shall last; for God loveth it. And even so hath everything being — by the love of God!'

This little book laid part of the foundation of our new religious life together. The Church with its concepts of heaven and hell and its morality code had lost its grip on us and something else took over at which we have worked to build on ever since.

On the way home we visited father's grave in Lauban/Silesia. The rose-bush that mother had planted had grown into a little tree and would be blossoming soon. And I showed Francis the place and the garden where I had spent the best part of my childhood and where I had been so happy. On the way from the

Francis and Madeleine with
Gretel and friend, Hamburg,
1941

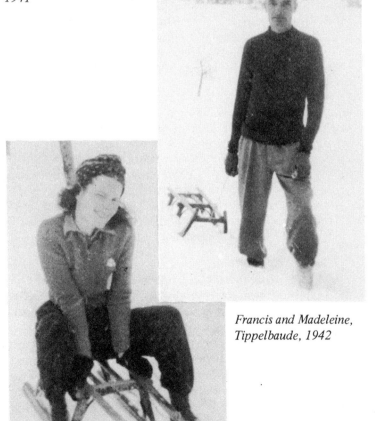

Francis and Madeleine,
Tippelbaude, 1942

cemetery we passed the fairground *(Rummelplatz)* were I won
that multi-coloured ball, and I told him the story. How shrunk
everything looked like from a toy-box.
   In July of 1943, Hamburg suffered the worst attack so far
known in this war. It had been planned and executed by Arthur
(Bomber) Harris and been meant, as all his other terrible
attacks, for the civilian population. These 'area bombings' were
to break the morale of the people and thus bring about a quick
end to the war. But it didn't work out like that. The morale of
the people was not broken. It went on for ten days, the RAF
attacked four times and the Americans twice. I mention this,
because my younger sister Gretel, who had been friends with
Frank Ryan the summer before, was then a nurse in Eppendorf
hospital, a huge modern complex just outside Hamburg. She
was one of the million refugees who had escaped that in-
cineration. About 42,000 Germans were killed. The devastation
on such a great scale was simply horrific. Her hospital and all
around it had disappeared from the earth. She came in a completely distraught state to Berlin, a nervous wreck with rags on
her body. I went with her to a friend who had at that time a
villa at the *Wannsee* to recover. And what happened in Hamburg
and what I experienced later in Berlin, and especially in Munich,
was the phenomenon known as a firestorm, accompanied by a
mighty roar. I quote here from Max Hastings "Bomber
Command":

> *As the fires reached incredible temperatures one thousand
> degrees centigrade and more — they sucked in the air and
> bellowed themselves into hurricanes of flames and smoke
> that tore through the heart of Hamburg amidst winds of
> 150 m.p.h.*

In February 1945 Arthur Harris, on Churchill's orders sent
his planes to bomb Dresden. It was no military target, but again
an area bombing just to create havoc amongst the inhabitants
and the thousands of refugees from the East, fleeing from the
Russians. Many who were not killed by bombs were burnt to
death in the firestorms.
   RAF Mosquito attacks on Berlin increased. Buildings
crumbled like sandcastles. More and more gaps yawned in the
streets and soon you could see miles and miles of the city

flattened out. It was difficult and dangerous to work under these circumstances, so the English and Irish Redaktion moved for safety's sake to Luxemburg. Work was carried on from the Luxemburg Sender. Francis went as he still gave his weekly talks to Ireland and I went with him as I introduced his talks. But anyhow Francis would not have left me in air-raid-riddled Berlin. We moved on August 12th, 1943.

Life naturally was pleasanter in Luxemburg, though we did not care too much for the bourgeois citizens and they very likely didn't take to us as intruders in their place either. There were, thank God, no air-raids and drink was no problem. Pink champagne was "the" usual drink. Imagine that! Any inferior meal tasted delicious when washed down with that drink. The surroundings of Luxemburg are lovely, gentle hills and I remember the meadows, outside of Mondorf covered in Autumn with autumn crocuses. They are bigger than our crocuses, very delicate and mauve coloured.

We also visited the town of Metz; and this was the first time I saw a typical French town, rather narrow, with cobbled streets, and pastel-coloured houses with those charming pale shutters.

These excursions were rare, because mostly I worked for the whole day in the library. I was the only visitor there. I met Francis usually for lunch. I think he was very homesick for Ireland at that time.

Around November 20th I had to go back to Berlin because of my studies. Francis came with me. On the night of November 22nd to November 23rd my sister Traute and her friend Martin, and Francis and I, were huddled around the tiled stove to keep warm and pre-celebrate my birthday on the 23rd when the sirens started wailing. As we lived on the ground floor we didn't bother to go to the air-raid-cellar. Yet on that particular night the RAF mosquitos had marked out with their lit flares ('christmas trees') our district, Wilmersdorf, for their target of destruction. It literally rained bombs right and left, we heard them swishing down. But as long as you heard them you would not be hit by them. The worst ones that hit you *(Volltreffer)* came unnoticed, and you didn't hear anything. There was just a big bang — and you'd had it. I had quite forgotten that the sound does not travel faster than the actual fall. For example, in thunderstorms you first see the lightning and then the thunder follows, and the greater the distance between these two the less dangerous the thunderstorm. So when the school next-door was hit by a *'Volltreffer'* we had no warning. Suddenly a wild storm smashed the windows open, tore the curtains, shook the foundation of the house, but left intact a little vase on the shelf. How we got into the cellar I don't remember. Apparently the brain cannot absorb any shock so quickly. We had a narrow escape, the wings of death had just touched and warned us. Still, during the air-raid, Martin and Francis went on top of the house to keep the flames of the burning building next-door from spreading over to our house. We made a chain to pass buckets of water to the men on top. They were very brave because the bombs were still falling. The smoke was thick and hurt the eyes so we had to wear gas-masks. There was dense smoke, wind and blazing houses all around. What an inferno. Francis had great difficulty in getting through the burning streets to his room in Rankestr., not too far from us, to see to his books and MSS.

Towards morning we gathered in our shell of a room, where in spite of all, we finished the bottle of wine from the previous evening which we had brought from Luxemburg for my birth-day. "Happy birthday to you, dear S". An intense will to survive the disaster befell us. And that is how my first prayer was born in me. Because prayer was then and still is for me the intensity of living. How strange and miraculous it seems to me that my soul started to live while the city around me was dying. I learnt in those days what prayer is all about, that it embraces my whole life, how it does not mean a few minutes praying here or there, in the mornings or in the evenings, and has nothing to do with what I actually say, but is a way of living in the presence of God.

That experience — horrible as it was — had in it its sweet blessing. We grasped something about life and death for which we had not been prepared before. More than ever we knew what we had in each other; more than ever it became clear to us in that 'dark night' where all could crumble to dust and was fleeting, one thing only remained and which we had to pursue: the way to Truth.

As soon as possible we returned to Luxemburg, now doubly glad to have some respite from the attacks at night, but specially glad that life had become more precious to us than ever before. (That joy in being alive and on this earth has been with me ever since up till this very day). To those inner blessings our hotel owner of the Pariser Hof, Monsieur Petit, added his own blessings in the form of a roasted goose on Christmas Eve. It was wheeled into my room with a bottle of champagne and all the other goodies and trimmings of a feast. But for that goose — delicious as it was — I was nearly raped. The fellow who had promised us the goose led me into a cellar, and didn't want any money — but wanted me instead. God Almighty! I got the fright of my life. With my utmost charm I persuaded him to postpone the sexual encounter for another day. The Luxemburgers in general struck me as rather perverse. They would sleep with three to four men and women in one bed together — and they made no secret of it, the honesty of which I liked. Fool that I was — I had never heard of such goings on.

Francis still suffered from homesickness, and wrote the following beautiful poem at Christmas:

Ireland

Over you falls the sea-light festive yet pale
As though from the trees hung candles alight in the gale,
To fill with shadows your day, as the dismal beat
Of waves, fills the lonely width of many a western street.
Bare and grey and yet hung with berries of mountain ash,
Drifting through the ages with tilted fields awash,
Steeped with your few lost lights in the long Atlantic dark
Sea-birds shelter, our shelter and ark.

We had to return to Berlin, air-raids or no air-raids. We made a lot of the moon now, as the bombers came on cloudy, overcast, moonless nights; *"Der Mond steht hoch und klar"* (The moon stands high and clear), thank God, sounded like music to our ears, and soon the radio would announce: *"Das Reichsgebiet ist frei von feindlichen Flugzeugen."* (The Reich is free from enemy planes). We would go to bed and wish each other a *'Gute Nacht'.*

My examinations started in early March. With them hanging

over me plus the constant alarms I became a nervous wreck. We didn't go any longer to our primitive cellar, but if there was enough warning and usually there were about ten minutes from the time the bombers crossed into Western Germany to Berlin — we ran quickly — to the 'Bunker' near Bahnhof Zoo in the Tiergarten. It was a monstrosity of a huge square block of reinforced cement, said to be soundproof (which it was, you couldn't hear anything) and bombproof. By now people were streaming into it, and FLAK personnel carrying ammunition went to the top of the building. So we seemed to be pretty secure with the *Abwehr* aiming at the enemy planes. One night amongst that crowd I passed out, suffering from claustrophobia. When I came round, there were Francis and my sister around me, we had even been given a special little room meant for accidents etc.

Francis had helped me a lot with the preparation for the different subjects. English wasn't so bad — I had got through Francis a different angle of certain writers and poets. But Professor Schirmer didn't mind. In his seminars he even welcomed a different point of view. But philosophy was my weak point. I had chosen Francis Bacon, but handed his work ·over to Francis, and he had to read it all for me and then explain it as simply as he could. Francis found Bacon refreshing with his love of detached investigation, of sticking to reality, of clarity. He actually was glad to have found him — and that through me! At least I passed in that subject, the others I managed surprisingly well, not with *"Sehr gut"*, but with *"gut"*. So I jumped with joy when we got the results after a few weeks. The different examinations took place mostly in cellars, as on March 8th, '44 we experienced the first daylight attack on Berlin.

During that time Francis was bombed out, his little room, the haven for us for so many evenings, devastated. His Jugoslav landlady had saved some of his belongings which he found in a heap in the street amongst them a gramophone, but we could not take it. Francis was lucky to find a room in the Pension Naumann, where he had stayed before. As we didn't want to be separated, especially during the heavy attacks by night, he got me a little room as well. The roof of the house which had suffered from incendiary bombs, had been flattened with boards — which we later found ideal for sunbathing.

In between the air-raids we now did very little, we were glad to sit in the sun and so grateful to have survived so far and been given another breathing-space until the next sirens went. To dream of another better life was out of question. You had to accept life as it was and come to terms with it and make the best of it. I thought that I might not come out of this hell alive, but be buried, like so many thousands, under the piles of rubble.

In those days of inner and outer eclipse in war-time Berlin, where the sun often remained hidden behind a layer of smoke and dust, it was love that seized me with all its joys and sorrows and made a completely different person out of me. Fear had gone, love became my vocation, as Francis de Sales says: "Everything must be done through love, nothing through fear." Once love moved in, I became a very joyful person. Has there ever been a person, possessing all the riches, except love, who was joyful?

I don't mean here the romantic love that soon ends in stalemate. No, the love I mean must change the whole world for you, must be the beginning and end, must be centred in Christ. I realised only again very late in life that in loving another person you actually love Christ in the other being. And so love, centred in Christ, is in reality an intense prayer. How happy that realisation made me. I had often felt a bit guilty that in loving Francis I had neglected Christ, that HE was shut out.

I also realised that love consists mainly in fighting our own selfish, greedy, possessive ego, and if there were moments when I failed in that fight I had finally to accept St Paul who said:

Charity suffereth long, and is kind; charity envieth not; charity seeketh not her own, is not easily provoked, thinketh no evil, but rejoiceth in the truth. Charity beareth all things, believeth all things, hopeth all things, endureth all things.

(St Paul)

Looking back at all these thoughts St Francis de Sales was a great help to me:

God is not so terrible for those who love Him. He asks

little of us because He knows how little we have . . . let us practice the little virtue of our littleness. For a small dealer a small basket.

That was exactly what I was given, this small basket, and as mental prayer was and still is difficult for me, I just turned all my life, love, work, joy, sorrow, reading, listening to music and even doing nothing — into a prayer. And I became happy going about with this little basket in my heart.

Frank Ryan had also left the flat near the Stadtpark and moved into a room in Fräulein Hildegard Lübert's flat in Grunewald. Due to the increasing air raids he could not be left on his own for long because of his progressive deafness, and she looked after him. He was seriously ill by now. The previous summer when his illness had started he had had to go to the Charité hospital. I thought it was a horrible place which was more like a prison. He had suffered a stroke. Then he was sent to a sanatorium in Loschwitz near Dresden. We visited him there on St Patrick's Day, 1944. It was a very beautiful place and Frank had a beautiful room with a view of the Elbe. The park, where we strolled for a while, was immaculately kept, and yet all the luxury could not hide the mortuary in the grounds, which we passed on our walk with him. He showed us his pulse, throbbing in his wrist and said, "We'll be in Ireland next year!" A short time afterwards he returned to Berlin and in the late spring of that year Francis and I took turns at looking after him, as Frl. Lübert had to work, sometimes even at night, because she was a Pharmacist. When she worked night shift one of us would have to stay there. I was often terrified during those vigils as Frank looked ghastly. When Francis came in the morning he would shave him, and the two men would make plans to go to Switzerland and from there to Ireland. Frank thought that he would marry me for convenience sake, so that I could cross the border legally as well. Once safely over we would immediately get divorced. But Francis and I knew that Frank would never again see Ireland. His homesickness was heartbreaking to watch. I have never seen anyone long so much for his homeland. I think the nearer you come to death the more homesick you become. Both men would speak so much about Ireland, conjuring up for me this green island, with its blue mountains and its whitethorn hedges in spring that I used to think of the very ancient lines:

Ich am of Irlande
And of the holy lande of Irlande.
God, Sir, pray I thee,
And for sainty charity,
Come and dance in Irlande.

In early June Frank began to get worse and he had to return to Loschwitz. The last painful and saddening help that Francis could give him was to help him dress, putting on his socks and shoes for him. He was got ready for his last train journey and Frl Lübert went with him. The government has reserved a whole compartment for them. We were never to see him alive again. He was hardly back in Loschwitz, when we received a telegram from Frl Lübert that Frank had died. On June 10th, 1944, he was buried in Loschwitz cemetery. We were among about twelve people at his funeral. How sad it was, so far from his beloved Ireland that he had longed for. Budge Clissmann saw to it that Frank got a tombstone with his name in Irish on it.

Some months previously, shortly after my examination, I had written to my younger sister who was a nurse near Danzig to see if Francis and I could come for a couple of weeks just to get some quiet nights and recover a bit from the nervous strain. That part of Germany hadn't had any air-attacks. But they suffered badly when the Russians took the town. Friends and teachers who hadn't escaped committed suicide rather than fall into the Russian hands. But I got a negative reply. She could not have us as mother, who was now staying with her, felt very bitter about Francis and me. But despite this we got some respite with a friend in Kreibau/Niederschlesien, which was at that time of the year, just before the start of spring, a very bleak countryside with a thin covering of new snow and heavy lorries rolling towards the Eastern front day and night. We mostly stayed indoors, in the warm sittingroom and read "The Interior Castle" by St Teresa of Avila, which was written by St Teresa at the Carmelite Convent of Toledo in 1577 in obedience to her superior who wished that towards the end of her life she might explain something about prayer to the young nuns of her order, or daughters, as she called them. She didn't feel adequate to undertake this task and begged the Lord to speak for her, and at that very moment she had the vision of the soul as a castle made out of diamonds and clear crystal with many rooms in it, just as in heaven there are many mansions and "prayer and reflection are the gateway into the castle." Her way of writing is similar to Christ's way of teaching in parables. It sounds very down to earth, nearly simple, but out of reach for most, and certainly for me. She said herself: "The Lord gives when He wills, as He wills and to whom He wills." So I felt the Lord did not "will" for me to enter any of the different mansions, not even the threshold of the first. And yet, when all is said and done, this great sixteenth century mystic does not, as is sometimes thought, only serve as a guide for those *far* advanced in prayer and holiness. Even in the most exalted passages of the "Interior Castle" she is only saying in her own way, and with similes taken from her very practical life, what Christ said in parables for those who came to listen to the words of Life. She concludes her book with these words:

My sisters, do not let us build towers without foundations, for the Lord does not consider so much the greatness of our deeds, as the love with which they are performed.

The summer of 1944 was very hot in Berlin. We spent a lot of the time on the roof sun-bathing, and made tentative plans for the future. There was plenty of time for reading and Francis introduced me to Dostoyevsky. I read "The Brothers Karamazov" and "Crime and Punishment" which made an indelible impression on me. I copied out the last paragraph of "Crime and Punishment", as I felt it would be of vital importance to me now and later. Raskolnikov is tried, on Sonja's advice, and sent to Siberia for seven years imprisonment. Sonja follows him there, and can sometimes visit him. The book ends with these words:

At the commencement of their happiness they were ready to look on these seven years as seven days. They did not know that a new life is not given for nothing; that it has to be

41

paid dearly for, and only acquired by much patience and suffering, and great future efforts.

With the constant attacks by air Berlin began to resemble more and more a moon-landscape with dusty desolate streets, piles of rubble on either side of which the *Ostarbeiter* (workers from the East) had to work, clearing away the bricks etc. They looked at us so forlorn, so lonely and so immensely sad with hungry eyes, but would never say a word. When we had some bread to spare we would give it to them which was actually forbidden. Most trees lining the Berlin streets had been destroyed, yet in the square in front of the pension where Francis and I lived the 'Linden trees' had so far escaped. There was still some *'grün wirklicher Grüne'*, as Rilke would say, some real green still left in this desert of dust. Francis was touched by their sight in all the destruction around and wrote the following poem:

> *I see from the Linden trees out in the square*
> *(I see without looking, with only a glance at them)*
> *Much more than from hours of people, of books, of talk*
> *How to pass through these deathly days, how to walk*
> *Over the earth, in my bloom and yet bare,*
> *Balanced above the earth on my own thin stem.*
>
> *In their loose centre, in their blown breast*
> *There is shadow, they slant their leaves to the sun,*
> *And are green, but within there is rest*
> *Beyond green, beyond words and worlds*
>   *Let's have done*
> *With the world and what comes of it, peace or unpeace*
> *It is time that into our breasts*
>   *we gathered the shade*
> *Of our own dark leaves, of our life; and in these*
> *were still and waited: brides of their Lord arrayed.*

('The Tree in the Square', Summer 1944)

On May 10th, 1944, the Englische Seminar was hit in a day attack, which solved Francis' teaching problems there and then.

The war situation was becoming worse, the Russians were advancing from the East. Francis became anxious about me, as I was from Polish parents. He tried to get permission from the *Auswärtige Amt* (foreign office) and the *Polizei* (police) to travel. To travel more than 75km. you needed special permission from the authorities, and in order to get it, he pretended that he had to go south, to the town of Landsberg in Bavaria, (where, of all places, Hitler had written *"Mein Kampf"!*) in order to fetch some important belongings. Fortunately, he met some sympathetic officials and was given the necessary documents for himself and his secretary (me) to go South. My sister's friend, Martin, who was on duty at the station *(Bahnhofspolizei)* had reserved two good seats for us on the train. And after a heartbreaking farewell from my sister Traute, who would not leave Berlin because Martin was on duty there, we left from *Anhalter Bahnhof*, and arrived early one September morning in 1944 in Munich, having never had any intention of going near Landsberg. Near the station there stood a wooden barracks in front of which people were queuing to get a room somewhere. They all looked bedraggled and exhausted and were, in fact, refugees from the East who had lost their homes and were, like Francis and myself now, homeless. I joined the queue, leaving Francis in the background as we soon realised that foreigners weren't welcome, and that Francis, with his halty, broken German, would not have had a chance of getting anywhere. The courteous manner to which he was used to in Berlin were gone here. Everybody for himself was the motto of the day in this fight for survival. Yet I did manage to get a ticket which gave us three nights in the hotel Schiller, beside the station, which had already been badly damaged by attacks.

Chapter 2

FLIGHT: MUNICH, AUTUMN 1944

And all the time the Lord went before them, by day a pillar of cloud to guide them on their journey, by night a pillar of fire to give them light, so that they could travel night and day. The pillar of cloud never left its place in front of the people by day nor the pillar of fire by night.

That hotel Schiller, sounded beautiful, but was a dilapidated and rather shaky place, with large cracks in the walls so that you could see into the next room. It would be a drafty place if it should survive the winter and the air-attacks, which it hardly had so far. Everything around that station had already had its share of bomb attacks. Anyhow for three nights at least we had a roof over our heads. We deposited our luggage and made for the *Englische Garten.* It was a lovely, sunny September day. So we sunbathed there and dozed off after our restless night-journey only to be woken by the now familiar sound of the wailing siren. We seemed to have come *"vom Regen in die Traufe",* from the frying pan into the fire. We dashed to the nearest bunker under the gallery of Modern Art at the edge of the Park. The American bombers came over the Alps and the radio announced: *"Feindliche Verbände über Kitzbühler Alpen,"* which meant they were heading for Munich. When the attack was over we looked round for eventual eating-places. The menus looked better than in Berlin, but you had of course to queue.

After the three days we had to look for somewhere else to stay, but we found nothing. So we took a chance and caught the train south of Munich and got out at a charming village called Wolfratshausen in the Isartal. How beautiful the landscape seemed to us, the mountains, river, woods and valleys were all so peaceful with no signs of air-raids. We were lucky in this place and got into a guesthouse for a few weeks — what sense of relief! How cosy were the old-fashioned feather beds with their billowing feather ticks. The food too was really good and here I ate for the first time *Scheiterhaufen* which consists of a layer of toasted bread, apples and raisin, baked in the oven and eaten hot with cream (if there was any). The weather kept fine so we enjoyed our walks in the countryside with the Alps in the distance. Here in Wolfratshausen I especially remember our pre-occupation with Wordsworth, perhaps being so close to nature. He was a comfort to us:

The world is too much with us; late and soon,
getting and spending, we lay waste our powers:
Little we see in Nature that is ours.
. . . For this, for everything, we are out of tune,
It moves us not. — Great God!

Towards the end of September we returned to Munich and even got two rooms in the pension *"Exquisite'* in Luitpoldstr, in Schwabing, on September 29th. There we could stay as long as we liked, which was a blessing. There was nothing 'exquisite' though about the pension, but we were close to the *Englische Garten* and even had a beautiful view on it. Here in Munich we soon worked out our routine, tooks walks in the *Garten* with its autumnal trees, and went for meals to the *'Chinesische Turm'* (Chinese Tower) run by Frau Rüger. She was a motherly type who had her special clientele and soon we became a part of that circle which meant in practical terms: better food and often a second helping. I speak so much about food, but we were constantly hungry. Then we would sit in a café, as our rooms were cold, and over a cup of black *"Malzkaffee'* read Meister Eckhardt and Rilke together. Both of them had to be explained in depth to me by Francis. I had got the books from the library, and am sorry that I ever returned them, especially Meister Eckhardt, as the library soon went up in flames. I copied the Duino Elegies, and have them still.

The Duino Elegies were rather difficult to grasp, for me

anyhow. But we worked through all the ten elegies, which didn't make a great impact on me, as I found them too cerebral. I prefered Rilke's poems instead. The general theme in the elegies is the transience of human emotions. To this transience is linked the death motif, the latter really gives significance to us in life. These two main themes run through the entire work. I got far more out of Meister Eckhardt. The worse outward life became and the more buildings crumbled to rubble heaps so that no stone was left on another, the more we had the need to build our own Jerusalem, our interior castle, which had to withstand the pressure of the world. In spite of the war — we were at peace:

Thus in so far as you dwell in God you dwell in peace,
and to the extent that you are distant from God are you
also from peace. Whatever dwells in God possesses peace!
So far in God, so far in peace.
(Eckhardt "Reden der Unterweisung")

I often felt like the *"Drei Jünglinge im Feuerofen"* (Three young men in a furnace), who instead of being burnt to death came out unblemished, glorifying God.

The *Englische Garten* was a great blessing to us, it was for me the most beautiful park I ever saw. We took walks there every day and admired the trees now changing to autumnal colours. Some trees began to change in layers starting from the bottom so that the top would still be green. Those trees were especially beautiful, growing by themselves with ample space to stretch out their branches. Rilke speaks of them: *"O, der ich wachsen will, ich seh hinaus, und in mir wächst der Baum."* (O, I who want to grow, I look out, and the tree grows in me.)

And then in the evening coming home from the restaurant there were the stars with their constellations. Suddenly they became alive and very important for us like the trees. It was a great joy to spot the evening and morning star, Sirius and Orion. It is a pity that nowadays I no longer live with them, being in the city. But in those days we needed them more than today. And what you need most will be given to you.

When the sirens sounded — day or night — we dashed to the *Englische 'Luftschutzgraben'* near the *Chinesische Turm.* It

46

certainly was not a 'Bunker', nor a deep cellar, but just a deep ditch reinforced with wooden beams. It was more a shelter from shrapnel and splinters than from any heavy bomb. Any bomb in the vicinity would have been the end of us. But we preferred it this way as we found the cellar in the *Pension Exquisite* unpleasant, with the pompous doctor's family who spread themselves out on rugs with a wireless, a thermos flask and sandwiches. They were hardly in the cellar before they started munching and gorging themselves. They were oblivious to anyone around, and looked so well-fed. In this *Luftschutzgraben* in the Park you heard and felt any bomb falling miles away. It was especially bad in winter when the ground was frozen. We always had the impression that the bomb must have exploded right over our heads. We naturally all became nervous wrecks. Often when we climbed out after an air-attack, a fire-storm (as I spoke of in the Hamburg attacks) would be howling. It came from a wall of fire beyond the *Englische Garten.* Munich was a sea of flames, smoke and roaring wind. What a terrible, eerie sight. It could have been the end of the world.

The winter was a bad one, as continental winters mostly are. We suffered from the intense cold as there was no heating in our rooms, no water supply any more, the pipes were either frozen or damaged, and we were constantly hungry. The windows were boarded up with cardboard, and for water we had to go down to the Park and firstly hack a hole in the crust of the river and then get the ice-cold water in a bucket and wash ourselves in it. When once I had got some lard from a friend in Denmark I asked our 'Exquisite' landlady, whether we could fry some bread in it on her electric cooker and she replied: she was sorry, but we could not use her cooker, it would be *'abgenutzt'* (used up). Nice Christmas gesture, I thought to myself. But Frau Rüger in the Chinese Tower exchanged the fat into *'Reisemarken'* (ration cards). But naturally one's fat on a piece of bread was better than any *'Essensmarken'* (travel ration cards).

Christmas Eve, which we celebrated, was a sorrowful affair. We had for supper some *'Gröstl',* a mixture of potatoes mashed with blood in a nearby café, with not even a second helping. That stuff was awful, yet tasted delicious when we were ravenously hungry. I could have swallowed the whole bowl. As we were walking home we met a row of unbleached wooden coffins being hurriedly driven past us.

Lord, give each his own death,
The death that grows out of a life
In which was love and sense and need.
What makes death alien and hard
Is when it is not our own, one that
Takes us before we are ripe for it.

(Rilke)

In my little room we climbed into bed in track-suit and coats, covered ourselves with the bedclothes and lay there in the dark, as the electricity had long since been destroyed, and waited for the next alarm. Yet bleak and hopeless as it looked around us, we were true to our 'Jerusalem'. I lit a stump of a candle behind a transparency depicting The Nativity and we sang the song for every Christmas, *"Stille Nacht, heilige Nacht"*. Then I played on my mouthorgan and we prayed together, at peace despite everything, and just glad to be alive and together.

Strictly speaking I should have been drafted into an ammunition factory, or something similar, for the rest of the war. But as I had fairly good English I was allowed to join a *'Dolmetscher* Schule' (Interpreters School) for English. We were trained there in case the English or Americans won the War and occupied Germany. I sometimes attended to make a good impression, but with the increasing air-raids the whole thing fizzled out as far as I was concerned. The transport in Munich was very erratic, as the tramlines were all destroyed and the little temporary railway (like a toy-one) which passed our pension could not function properly. But we all enjoyed riding in it with its puffing engine.

The war gathered speed, attack followed attack, and streets crumbled around us like a pack of cards. Dresden, as I said before, got it especially bad in February, 1945. That city was teeming with refugees from the East. But Churchill ordered the attack and Sir Arthur Harris executed this devilish blanket bombing in which a hundred to two hundred thousand people were killed either by bombs or in the firestorm. And all this in two nights and a day. I thought of the parable "The possessed of Gerasa" in which an evil spirit goes into a herd of swine who hurl themselves in sheer madness down the slope into the sea.

Before leaving Munich on March 1st 1945 I had a prophetic,

48

really lovely dream. I saw us walking over hills and valleys, always towards the West following a bright star in the sky. We got tired and exhausted on that journey, but did not give up, believing in the guiding star. And then — it stopped, stood still over a white-washed place, somewhere in the West. We had reached our goal and this was to be our resting-place for good.

Christ once said to his disciples: "But pray ye that your flight be not in the winter." Ours unfortunately was which made it all the worse. The journey from Munich was a nightmare, beset by difficulties from the very beginning. The railway would not take our big suitcase, so we just dumped it in the luggage department addressed to *"Lindau"* and hoped for the best. Then I was not allowed to travel more than 70km, although Francis could still go to his legation in Bregenz. So we just boarded a train and hoped that no one would come and inspect the tickets. It was a drafty old train with no windowpanes left, and only cardboard instead. Naturally there was no heating. We didn't risk the whole journey but got out at Kaufbeuren and decided to walk from there to Kempten. We plodded along in atrocious conditions, in storm, sleet and rain. That countryside is anyhow known for its rough climate, and therefore called *"Die Rauhe Alp"* (The rough Alps). After 10km. we had to give up, and completely exhausted rested at the edge of a wood, where we ate some of the cutlets and drank some wine that Frau Rüger from the *Chinesische Turm* in the *Englische Garten* had given us for the journey. It was a most desolate place — I had never seen such bleakness before. But as we wondered how to go on from there a lorry appeared in the distance and Francis mustered all his courage, held out his arm and asked for a lift. Usually I did this kind of thing, but at that moment there was no spark left in me. The driver took us 30km. to Kempten, for which he got our last bottle of wine as money would have been no good. From there we still had to get to Bregenz. By then we didn't care any more and boarded a train, inspector or no inspector. This was repeated over and over again; drafty old trains, with windowless compartments, and then the endless waiting for other trains which came as they liked, often held up by alarms, while we waited cold and hungry. And when we finally reached Bregenz — what a disappointment!

Bregenz, city of so much later pain and heartbreak, as no other place had ever in store for us. Yes, Mr Cremin of the Irish Legation was there with his family in one of the hotels. He tried his best for Francis, but could really do nothing in these chaotic times. He entertained us lavishly. It was a real peace-time lunch with the best wine and *Apfelstrudel* and real coffee. He gave us an introduction to a certain Herr von Schönbeck in Lindau, a very unpleasant looking individual, who was eager to meet Stuart and help him if possible. But when we did meet him it became evident that there was a mix-up. The situation became very embarrassing for Francis. Herr von Schönbeck had a Baily Stewart in mind, the infamous captain in the Scots Guards who was imprisoned in the Tower for treason shortly before the war after having been on leave in Berlin, and dismissed from the British Army in disgrace. After his release he went back to Germany and became a protégé of the Nazis for whom he broadcast anti-British propaganda to England. After the war he was tried and was given a rather lenient sentence. He might have been a double agent. He said at the trial: "My bark was worse than my bite." After his short sentence he came to Dublin where he died. Naturally Herr von Schönbeck was deeply apologetic but could not help us.

All the places around Lake Constance were teeming with refugees of all kinds of nationalities, rich and poor. They hoped to enter the 'Promised Land' of Switzerland which very few did, certainly no poor people. The rich ones had a chance. We were allowed to stay again for only three nights in a little hotel and then again *"Weitergehen"* (move on). People were moved from one place to another, no one could settle anywhere. We were like bees whose beehive had been disturbed and interfered with. It was especially bad for Francis because as a foreigner he was not allowed to be within 15km. of the border. So I thought of a place outside that limit which my Spanish teacher in Berlin had recommended and where she herself had spent some holidays. The woman was Spanish, the husband German, and they had a few children.

On Monday, March 5th 1945, we started for Tuttlingen. But our train didn't go that far, because of low-flying aeroplanes scouring roads and railway-lines and shooting at anything moving. That was why of late, trains only went by night in complete blackout. We had to get out shortly before Tuttlingen and take shelter in a drafty waiting-room. The cold was terrible. We spent the night there. At daybreak we made for Tuttlingen, leaving our heavy leather suitcase which had actually arrived at Lindau station, in the 'left-luggage' office. That beautiful heavy thing, a souvenir from Ireland, was in one way a real nuisance on our flight, yet it contained all that we possessed on this earth. To our surprise the Liebermann family took us in, my Spanish teacher had left, so her little room on top of the house was empty. My God, we were so relieved to have a roof over our head! Frau Liebermann was quite nice, especially when we handed her all our ration cards and the extra ones which we had always kept in reserve from Martin in Berlin. Francis got a little cart and fetched the suitcase. We could now wash and put on a change of clothes. The atmosphere in the family was not too pleasant as they were constantly bickering. The husband was completely cowed by his Spanish wife, who looked with her raven-black hair like a witch and whose voice was harsh and piercing like that of a parrot. We got a bit apprehensive. Food was scarce so Frau Liebermann and I went into the country begging for bread. It was hard to come by and I felt very humiliated. We would sooner have starved than be exposed to hard unpleasant country folk. We had met others on our flight and had found them all very mean; once when I had asked for the apples on the ground I was scolded and not given a single one. How greedy in general they were. But we were glad when we returned home for the first time with our rucksacks filled with that delicious manna. But soon those excursions came to an end. Diary March 22nd: "Out in the country yesterday looking for bread and not getting any. Walked 20km., returned home more hungry than when setting out."

But once our extra ration-cards had come to an end things changed for the worse for us. We were no longer welcome. Suddenly they pretended to be afraid of having given Francis shelter, should the victorious allies come. So we avoided them as much as possible and ate out and spent most of the days in cafés or in the nearby wood. The weather had changed, Spring was in the air, the days got warmer and we even could sun-bathe. There is a lovely incident, amongst all the harshness, which meant a lot to us. One day when we were sunbathing in the wood we saw a black snake creeping out of its winter

51

hideout, onto a flat stone. And there it stayed, blinking with its bright eyes, its metallic body absorbing the warm sun. We watched in awe and didn't dare to move unless we disturbed this sweet harbinger of Spring and of hope.

Whenever we entered the kitchen to get the key, one of the Liebermann's would say something disagreeable, and tell us to get out of the place. My diary on Easter Monday 1945 reads: "What a nightmare. These people wanting to put us out — shouting at us and now are not speaking and we have nowhere to go. What a terrible Easter for all of us. On the table in front of us we have Fra Angelico's picture of the Resurrection with the words at the bottom of it: *"In der Welt habet ihr Angst. Aber seid getrost, Ich habe die Welt überwunden."*

So we left Tuttlingen on Friday, April 6th 1945, without knowing where to go. We tried to get in here and there, but all in vain. So we had to sleep in waiting-rooms, spend the days in the woods near Lake Constance, and stay constantly on the move, as Francis could not remain longer than twenty-four hours near the *"Grenzzone"* (frontier zones). Fortunately for all of us refugees, it was a glorious Spring. I have never seen such a Spring in such profusion of blossoms as there. All the slopes towards the lake were covered with cherrytree blossoms — it was one huge white veil. We spent the days in the woods near Lindau, where I would do some washing in the stream and we would eat our three slices of bread for lunch and two for supper. The eating-out had become a problem, as we had no *Essenskarten,* not being registered in Lindau, and not daring to be registered because Francis was a foreigner. Sometimes I was lucky and could exchange a few cigarettes for bread from soldiers. How glad we were when sometimes a soldier had to catch a train, and could not finish his meal, and pushed the plate towards us. Or was there no train to catch and had he just taken pity on our hungry eyes watching him eat?

On our wanderings near the Bodensee we met many high-ranking French people. They were well-dressed, and so far hadn't suffered any hunger. Once in the waiting-room of Lindau station as we sat at a table with a cup of black *Ersatz-kaffee* in front of us, we saw a most wonderful sight that cheered us up and was a balm to our hearts. On the table quite close to us sat a Siamese cat, being fed with titbits by its

52

owners. After finishing his meal he took to cleaning and licking and washing himself, his dark-brown paws and muzzle, completely unperturbed by the chaos around him. How his owners must have loved him, and at the same time feared for him. We only hoped that God would protect that little creature, so innocent, in a world full of evil. I didn't know then that in a few years' time Francis would make me a present of just such a Siamese kitten.

The nights in the Lindau *Wartesaal* with its teeming mass of refugees were horrible. This waiting-room with its white benches had seen better times, when passengers waited here for a steamer to take them for a cruise on a lake, perhaps with a stop on the shores of Switzerland? Our side of the lake was pitch-dark, but across the lake in Switzerland a profusion of lights glittered and taunted us. So near the 'Promised Land' and yet so far! Here on this side all was dark and filthy with people sleeping in the dust on the floor and forever scratching themselves. If no-one else had a good time, fleas and lice certainly did. We both were frightened of these little bugs and could not find rest. Our heads lolled from one side to the other: "The foxes have holes, and the birds of the air have nests, but the son of Man has nowhere to lay His head."

Occasionally the police swooped down on us, and woe to him or her who couldn't prove with a railway ticket that they were only spending the night there. They took Francis one night and searched him from top to bottom. I thought I would never see him again. I had such a disgust for these people, I could have murdered the lot of them! There is a town not far from Lindau called Wangen, its name is written with indelible ink in my mind, where the people in the *Stadthaus,* where we applied for ration-cards, treated Francis like an outcast, the worst of criminals. They behaved as if Germany was winning the war, so brutal, so beastly. And here I have to say something after long thought and many years. But I did write it in my diary at that time. I know that if you visit these places today, as a tourist — and especially Southern Germany — you are welcomed with *"Grüss Gott"* here and there, in fact they smother you with it. But be in need, in desperate need, and they have hearts of stone. Their *"Grüss Gott"* is all on the lips, but not in the heart where it should be. Christ hated these Pharisees. That's why you have to suffer, be an outcast in a place and then, and only then, will you really know the people.

We had to find a place, if possible a camp, where at least I could stay. We could no longer carry our suitcase and heavy winter-coats. The war dragged on, the midday bulletins in the windows were all the same, and although the Russians were advancing towards the Oder, the Germans were still thinking of winning. Quite desolate we leaned against the wall at the lakeside and looked towards Switzerland. With nothing else to do, we took a train to the South of Lindau to a place called Dornbirn. It was April 16th, 1945, and this place seemed empty to us. So we came back on the following day, April 17th and — lo and behold! — I got into the NSV camp for refugees. Francis, of course, was not taken. But at least I had a bunk, and we could deposit the heavy suitcase and get *Essenskarten*. I didn't have to give up any ration cards so Francis could have them, but unfortunately he still had to roam about. There were quite a few bunks empty so on a dark night I would smuggle him in, and he could at least sleep in peace.

On Sunday night, April 22nd, he left for Lindau to spend the night there and then go a bit further and return on Tuesday. Had we known that the allies were so near we would never have parted. Francis had hardly gone when in the late evening we heard shooting, the French were near Lindau! Panic broke out and many refugees left the camp going towards the Swiss border. I felt like it too — but waited and waited for Francis to come back. Whenever the door opened I imagined that he was about to enter. Monday dawned — time passed — but no Francis came. I got so worked up that I could not stay any longer in the place and walked towards the Swiss border. About eleven o'clock I returned and found to my incredible joy that Francis was waiting for me. We packed a few things in a hurry and made for the border to the town of Feldkirch. On the way there he told me why he had been so late arriving. As it happened it was only luck that we were still together. When Francis was walking along the shore of Lake Constance (as the trains had ceased running) he was halted by a German soldier who prevented anybody from going further. There was chaos on the lakeside with the rumbling of the French guns in the distance. When Francis pleaded with him and showed him his out-of-date Irish

54

passport, the soldier couldn't make anything out of it, but went to his superiors and showed him the strange document. The officer in charge came out with a large grin over his face and remarked to Francis how extraordinary it was to meet a compatriot of one of his favourite writers, Ernie O'Malley, whose book, 'On Another Man's Wound', he had read and enjoyed so much. O'Malley had fought on the same side as Francis in the Irish Civil War. There was no question now of not letting Francis through and so he was able to meet me safely because of that miraculous incident.

A long queue of refugees waited to be let in at the checkpoint in Feldkirch; their papers were checked and mostly they were not accepted, practically no one was allowed in, even Pétain and Pierre Laval had been turned back − and so were we. Marshal Pétain and Pierre Laval had headed the German-sponsored French Government at Vichy in unoccupied France at the time of the French capitulation in 1940. Pétain had been a Marshal of France and Laval a Minister in pre-war French Government. Towards the end of the war they and other members of the Vichy Government were brought to Sigmaringen in Germany as a so-called French Government-in-exile. Later they tried to get to Switzerland, as I said, but were turned back; Laval was executed by order of General de Gaulle at Fort Valérien outside Paris in 1945. He had tried to commit suicide, but did not succeed and was carried unconscious to the execution yard. Pétain was imprisoned on an island off La Rochelle.

We tried a second time for Switzerland on April 24th with the same negative result. They might have let Francis in, but I was the obstacle. They scrutinised Francis' passport, took it into the hut, but came back with the answer that I was not the legitimate wife. Francis had put me in his passport. In utter dejection we sat near the barbed wire in the wood and ate all of our sandwiches in despair − with the dogs barking on the side of the fence. We had hit rock-bottom very hard and wondered would we ever come up again.

But we did, at least for the time being. I got a little room with Frau Fussenegger whose son was fighting at the front, and whose room was not used. It was on the ground floor, and had its own entrance − there were no words to describe our joy!

55

Francis kept a low profile, but Frau F. did not mind him and actually promised him a room on top of the house. In the meantime he would have to go to a camp outside of Dornbirn to sleep. The Fusseneggers were caretakers for the bank on the ground-floor.

A couple of days before the French marched into Dornbirn the shops suddenly opened the floodgates. Overnight there was plenty of food. We queued here and there, and in the end we had managed to get several loaves of bread, pounds of cheese, maze flour, sugar and other things. But all this had to last for a long time, because it took quite a while after the French took over before life became normal again. And then the real hunger started. It was a very strange sight when the French rolled in on their tanks and lorries to see the town so desolate, with nobody about, and only white flags and sheets greeting the soldiers. It was the beginning of the long-awaited peace. Extract from Francis' diary:

May 2nd, 1945
"On May 2nd 1945 at half-past one French troops occupied this town. For us the long years of war, one special phase of our life was over. What a month of horror April had been! From Easter to the end: sleeplessness, three weeks without undressing or washing, without a bed, cold and hungry. We mostly had five slices of doughy bread with a bit of butter or margarine. Then there was the anxiety of being taken, being searched. And yet in spite of all that — what a month of miraculous revelations never to be forgotten."

I know we were desolate when we were refused entry into Switzerland which meant for us 'the Promised Land'. But we had to accept it, and not lose faith. We would sit under the white cherry blossoms on the sunny shores of Lake Constance and gaze beyond to the land of freedom and plenty. But anyhow we had been extremely lucky to get the little room with such fine people as the Fusseneggers. We could not have met with kinder people whether mother, father or daughter. I got from Frau F. a missal which I still use and as there were no other books available only the Old and New Testament and the Psalms, we made the most of them. These few weeks that followed now were the most important ones in my life. I think

56

all the miseries and trials would have been wasted on me (if not on Francis), had I not been given the quiet hours of reading the Bible and the psalms and of pondering over them. Many of the psalms I copied and learnt by heart. For my parched soul it was *the* nourishment I needed. For hours we used to sit at the open window of Francis' attic — which he now had got from Frau F. and read the psalms. How beautiful and blessed it was to be able to sit at last in peace without being harrassed and pushed here and there. We literally only had to lift up our eyes to the white, snow-clad mountain range across the river Rhine to get the meaning of the psalm: "I will lift up mine eyes unto the hills; from whence cometh my help." For us it was no longer any mountain, nor any river we were beholding, but Mount Hermon, the "singular mountain" and the river Jordan. Like the old Jews we could lament our fate: "O my God, my soul is cast down within me; therefore will I remember thee from the land of Jordan, and from the Mount Hermon, the unique mount."

And although "deep calleth unto deep, his waves and water-falls all pour roaring over me," we need not despair, there was a glimmer of hope for us, as the psalmist goes on to say: "Yet by day the Lord encompasses me with his mercy, and at night his song remains with me, a prayer unto the God of my life." These comforting, soothing words which gently reassured my anxious soul have remained one of my favourite prayers up till today. "Why art thou cast down, O my soul? and why art thou disquieted within me? Hope thou in God; for I shall yet praise him, who is the healer of my soul, and my God."

When I was saying the psalms I was always struck by the intense feeling of the Jews. The relationship with God was such an urgent one, God lived literally by day and night in front of them, when they wandered through the desert. Miracles would happen then which could not happen now, as the miracle of faith had to be first in them, before it could manifest itself in outward ways, like the raining from heaven of manna and the gushing forth of fresh water from the desert-rock.

This recalls a little incident in my life. It was the end of the war and we were walking along a dusty, deserted country road. We were very hungry, so hungry indeed that I thought I could not go on any further. Just then my eyes spotted two crisp fresh rolls right under my feet: How did they get there? Had a lorry of the victorious French army laden with food passed by and lost some of its precious contents to fall into my lap? Be it as it may, the incident was miraculous for us. This manna didn't only strengthen our body but lifted up our spirit in wonder and gratitude at God's infinite tender, gentle ways of caring for us. "The Lord is my shepherd I shall not want."

It seems as if all the outer happenings of the Jews like exile, wandering, captivity — haunting as they are in their own way — are really only the scenery for our inner captivity and exile. In spite of all the outward comings and goings the essence of them is: stillness in God. "My soul, wait thou only upon God; for my expectation is from Him."

One miracle after the other was showered on us. People, unknown to us, would leave potatoes, tins of sardines, vegetables and other things at the door. Frau F. would often come down with a thick bean-soup. We were not meant to despair. We knew that great blessings — inward and outward ones, were given us, but also knew that we had to pay for them in the past, but also would have to pay in the future and that these blessed weeks were given to us to gather enough strength and faith for future trials awaiting us.

Here is an extract from Francis' diary:

Dornbirn, June 3rd, 7.45 p.m.
"Sitting in S's small room after our supper of three slices of bread and butter, a few radishes and tea. S. lying in her bed reading. A deeply peaceful day, like those that have gone before, like the whole of last month in spite of the shadow, the uncertainty and the more or less continual hunger. Oh, if I could go there (Ireland) and bring S. and live secretly, out of the world and do my work again and be a source of peace to those around me as I was often not before."

On the next day (4th) we were in Feldkirch about my business of reaching France with Francis. In pouring rain, drenched to the skin, we walked along the road to the camp with little hope in our hearts. In the camp we saw a lot of Red Cross parcels piled up high, and mountains of chocolate and loaves — those white French ones. We could have done with some of them — we were as usual hungry — but nobody even thought that two miserable wet creatures could even feel anything like hunger, especially not that fat busy monk who acted as interpreter — a priest of the worst sort, not to be compared to the fine French chaplain in Dornbirn, who said Mass early every morning in the main church there. This one was huge and fat and his face was shining, probably from a hearty breakfast of rashers, sausages and fried eggs, with toast. He had just finished a pious address to the French who were clasping their hands like in prayer. It struck me as being all very phoney. We achieved nothing there — which was obvious from the very beginning. It was strange that whenever a person or an atmosphere struck us as unpleasant, we never achieved anything.

How much better was our French adjutant Rieper in Dornbirn who gave us 120 cigarettes the day before which we used as exchange. Unfortunately he left Dornbirn soon afterwards. It is strange to think that he and Francis would discuss James Joyce.

D'n June 16th, 45:
"Yesterday we spent a beautiful day. Francis finally got his bed in the attic. The camp near Dornbirn where he spent the nights were horrible. They treated him like a Ukrainian worker. I decorated the room with the pictures from our Berlin time: Césanne's dark brooding trees, the Irish cottages from the Western coast and Francis' tramp that he had drawn for me."

June 18th, 45:
"Beautiful days, we got peas and potatoes. Through all these blessings we try to get strength for the coming time, as there is always Francis' fate looming over us. What will they do with him?"

D'n 21st, 45:
"Was at Mass with Francis early in the morning, then did a bit of shopping. Heard the peace-news, which gave me a horror because of the fear of separation. I am thinking that Francis should go to Ireland and get me over from there. But what would I only do without him? What a shadow is hanging over us — and yet what peace we have in spite of all.

> *Yea, though I walk through the valley of the shadow of death,*

59

I will fear no evil; for Thou art with me;
Thy rod and thy staff they comfort me.

(Psalm 23)

"Today there is such lovely June weather, all is rich and in full blossom. There are those white lilies growing in the garden, which don't spin nor worry, but even Solomon in all his splendour wasn't clad like one of them."

D'n June 27th, 45:
"Today Francis went to Lindau to speak with a British colonel about our return. It is like a nightmare — if only he would come back."

D'n June 29th, 45:
"Francis returned safely from Lindau. But my return gets more and more difficult. What will become of us? The mountain ashes have already yellow berries and soon they will be red and what then? Again another winter in misery?"

July 1st, 1945:
"Discovered today the psalm *"An den Strömen Babels sassen wir da und weinten"* what great joy that is and at the same time "The Canticle of Cantiles". in an anthology that Frl. Wimmer had lent us. The copying and learning them by heart has no end. I will have need for them in future time when I have no books and have to rely on my memory. We include these especially in our daily prayers."

D'n July 11th, 45:
"We spend our days in peace and try to have *"Geduld"* as Rilke said: *"Ich lerne es täglich, lerne es unter Schmerzen, denen ich dankbar bin, Geduld ist alles."* (I learn it daily, learn it under pain, for which I am grateful, patience is all.")

D'n August 3rd, 45:
"My God — what a change! Yesterday Francis was in Bregenz, and was told to live in the camp there and be ready for a transport to France. From Paris he will contact Ireland and try to get me over. So we returned to Bregenz yesterday with his luggage. The farewell was frightful. Now in a few moments I will be on my way in the train to Bregenz again to see Francis.

He worries a lot at leaving me behind. I have hardly ever seen him crying. But he knows that I am well looked after with the Fusseneggers. The last week we spent with Frl. F. she was ill. We prayed together and listened to music. How he loved this little room here — his dormitoir in the camp did not look nice. How glad I will be to see him in an hour's time. It is a very short train journey from D'n to Breg. What happiness that will be to see him, hear him, feel him, to take his Tiger paw. Oh Tiger . . . "

D'n August 5th, 45:
"Today we had one of the finest days — Tiger came down from Bregenz for the afternoon. There are no transports in the afternoons — usually towards evening, or most likely during the night and early morning. I had made a delicious *Apfelstrudel* under the guidance of Frau Fussenegger. She also gave me a white table-cloth, cake-forks and even napkins. I had picked some roses in a vase, then I had copied some of our favourite psalms and made them into a little book (which Francis still has — a bit worn from great use) and then I had knitted a pair of socks in three different colours, but never mind, they were whole and warm. We finished the whole cake! Later before supper we prayed and read Rilke's poem:

He was beset by fears that were deathly and undendurable.
Slowly he taught his heart acceptance as he might have
    brought up a son.

(Free translation)

Tiger looks well, as the food in the camp, run by French staff, is quite good and really ample; he even has red wine. I am anxious to see him tomorrow again."

All the time whether we roamed the roads or felt forlorn, hungry and miserable we had the comfort of the psalms and then we still had each other. At that time Francis was at least in the camp in Bregenz awaiting a transport for Paris. He only came down twice to Dornbirn so as not to be too long away from the camp. So every day I took a train and we used to meet at the entrance of the station. With what trepidation would I hurry to the entrance, wondering would he still be there? Francis was taller than the rest of the waiting crowd, so I could spot him immediately. We spent our last precious hours together on the shores of Lake Constance with a heavy heart. It might be the last afternoon for us together. We spoke little, as everything that could be said had been said.

Later in the afternoon we would go to the café Montfort where we had a cup of black *Ersatzkaffee* and Francis always offered me some round whitish biscuits he had saved for me from his ration. They tasted of nothing — but to me coming from him they were like manna! I in turn would then read out in a whisper some of our psalms we loved. No one took any notice of us, although the place was teeming like a bee-hive with all kinds of dispossessed people.

When I reached Bregenz on the 11th of August Tiger was not at the station. I hurried to the café, not there; then to the camp, not there either. Somebody else lay on his bunk, and his neighbour told me that he had left this morning at 2 o'clock with a transport. He had left me a short note saying he did not know the previous evening about the transport and that his coat and book were in the office with a note and cigarettes. I had a terrible nightmare on the night before. In it there was a chalice with hosts that someone held, but the chalice was too heavy and all the precious hosts cascaded to the ground. Was that the hour when he had left? We had prayed that last afternoon specially fervently on the Gospel of the wheat grain that must die to bring hundred-fold fruit and said the poem by Rilke "The Saint". And although I had prepared myself so much for this hour when it finally happened I could not take it in and would not believe that he had gone; I went on seeking everywhere in the town, along the streets, along the shore, in the cafés and back to the camp, wondering was he still waiting for me at the railway entrance and had I missed him? Back I went but nobody was there:

> *Oh my dove, that art in the clefts of the rock,*
> *In the secret places of the stairs, let me*
> *see thy countenance, let me hear thy voice,*
> *I will seek him whom my soul loveth,*
> *I sought him, but I found him not.*

The following entries in my diary, which I wrote practically every day, are very repititious. Each day was the same long constant wait for news from Francis. There was no post as yet which made it all the worse for us. But we did manage to get an address in Switzerland through Frau Fussenegger, who knew somebody who went there occasionally and could collect mail, if it hadn't got lost on the way. All was so uncertain, but at least I could write and hope to hear from Francis one day.

D'n, August 13th, 45:
"Yesterday was a hard day. In the evening I went for a walk with the Fusseneggers. In the sky we saw the first quarter of the new moon. It is said to be lucky. Would Francis see it too, somewhere en route to Paris and think of all the times when we saw it together. How often did we see it in the *Englische Garten* in Munich. The days seem endless now — I wish I could bundle time away. I have never felt so desolate in my life, as if all my energy is gone. 'My God, my God, why hasth thou forsaken me?' I have found a beautiful French prayer which I will learn by heart. One line goes as follows:

Have pity on them who loved each other and who are
*   separated.*
Have pity on the Objects of our tenderness . . .

D'n August 16th, 45:
"A week ago tomorrow we spent our last day together. It was pouring rain outside, but the Café Montfort was a haven for us. You had such a lot of biscuits and white bread and cigarettes for me. I was so glad with all these things that you said, 'Perhaps later when I can buy you lots of things, there would never be that joy.' You thought so, but you are not right. My joy in you is always there and can never diminish. Six days you are gone now and it seems more like six years. Time goes crawling like a snail."

August . . . :
"Beloved, I have just got a letter from you. Frau Fussenegger brought it down. What immense joy! I can't grasp it. How beautiful it all seems. Many, many thanks, my love."

August . . . :
"It is now a fortnight since you were here, in this little room. Today I finished copying out the psalms. I wish I could tell you how I am cared for, both inwardly and outwardly. I am practically never hungry and inwardly am not in despair. I have learnt some *'Geduld'* (patience). In the evening when I get lonely I look at your photo on the sleigh in the *Tippelbaude* where you smile, a bit mischievous, and then I must smile as well. And a time once again will come when I shall be saying 'I held him tight and did not let him go.'

August . . . 45:
"Saturday — as usual a lot of cleaning. I help Frau F. scrub all the stairs. Then made an *Apfelstrudel,* and afterwards again saw the doctor. It is nothing special, I think it is all nerves, the after-effect of the war. In the afternoon I went with the Fusseneggers to their allotment and picked apples. Now it is evening, I have had my tea and smoked a cigarette. It was again a hard day, trying to bear all with *'Geduld',* by accepting all, it is a prayer without words. The psalms are a great help to me. And that we discovered them in the last moment — what blessing that was. I must always think of the Israelites: 'The Lord hath done great things for us.' I try not to lose trust in God, I try to believe that HE leads us on the right path."

D'n Aug. 20th, 45:
"Three weeks ago Tiger and I spent our last evening together. Autumn is coming. Day and night there is rain. I am surprised at the constant rain and rather early autumn. The meadows are all covered with autumn crocuses which I saw for the first time in Mondorf near Luxemburg, a year later in Wolfratshausen and now in Dornbirn. They are so fragile. I'm allowed to stay here in Austria until end of December, then have to go back to Germany. Every entry in my diary starts since you left: 'Thank God again another day over', am glad to go to sleep and hope to dream of you."

D'n Aug. 26th, 45:
"Soon another day over — how glad I am. I dreamt the other night of him, his mouth was so sore. I dream so often, but never see his face really, just more or less the atmosphere.

All things which I evaded facing like T's departure and the uncertainty have happened to me sooner or later. What I mean is: what one is afraid of will happen to one, what one isn't afraid of, won't happen. But I feel that forever will I be afraid of losing Francis. Oh, these dark days without a glimpse of hope."

D'n Aug. 27th, 45:
"Again another day over. Thank God! — but no news from Tiger. I saw today some fine sunflowers. I love them best of all flowers. We read it together in the Berlin days: 'Ah sunflower, weary of time, who countest the steps of the sun; seeking after that sweet golden clime where the traveller's journey is done.' (Blake). Helped Frau F. a bit. She knocked at my door and probably doesn't like it that I'm so much alone. Anyhow she said that I shall soon get post from Francis. I think a lot of our walks in the *Englische Garten.* How I miss them. In general I long for Munich. I wouldn't mind the ruins. I feel a ruin myself. How beautiful the golden trees in autumn were, and later in winter the bare trees with the pale moon at the dark sky! 'The heavens declare the glory of God; and the firmament sheweth his handy work.' (Psalm 19)

Darling, where are you, how is it with you? Goodnight."

D'n Sept. 2nd, 45:
Again a lonely Sunday. How glad I am that it is over. It was especially lonely as all the Fusseneggers were out until now (that is 9 o'clock in the evening). Frl. Martha just brought me a cup of milk and two slices of bread with thick butter on them. That did me good as I had a very poor lunch, then in despair ate a lot of apples. In the afternoon played the record we liked so much, that Kyrie of the Mass, G Major by Mozart. I played it three times.

In the morning heard a Russian Mass in St. Franziskus, with beautiful Russian chanting. What haunting voices they have. Yesterday Frl. M. gave me the hope that letters might still come as the fellow goes very seldom into Switzerland — once or twice a fortnight. But I have no hope. From day to day I miss him more — no help and comfort from God as if completely forsaken. How glad am I when I only hear the footsteps of F. above me — and there in the mornings I can speak a bit —

but that is all. I thought this afternoon that I would go mad. Why did I ever let Francis go? Yet in spite of my feeling forsaken I pray for the right way for me: 'Show me thy ways, o Lord; Teach me thy paths, Lead me in the truth, and teach me: for thou art the God of my salvation.' (25) "

D'n Sept. 4th, 45:
"It is a rainy autumn evening. I passed the day quietly reading, some French poems by Verlaine and then I came on the 'Joseph Story' in the Old Testament. So far I didn't like the Old Testament, where they are only getting children etc. But Joseph is beautiful, the one who was the apple of Jacob's eye, and for whom he had made the coat of many colours. That story moved me to tears.

Am reading now the exodus of the Jews from Egypt, where they had stayed 430 years in all. How they had suffered in the foreign country, what longing for their Zion, what a close relationship they had with the Lord. He practically lived amongst them. He forgave them time and again when they rebelled against Him, He fed them with Manna and gave them drink. How glad would I be if I could wander with Tiger towards our promised land. 'And the Lord went before them by day in a pillar of cloud to lead them the way, and by night in a pillar of fire . . . and He took not away the pillar of cloud by day nor the pillar of fire by night from before the people.' (Exod.) Good night, *den mein Seele Liebt.*"

D'n Sept. 10th, 45:
"Today a letter from Francis! What a fine one! Oh, how glad I am. Nothing could have made me more happy than to hear that he is alright. What a weight off my chest. When I sit in the evening at the window I often imagine he might appear at it and beckon to me:

> *Behold, he standeth behind our wall,*
> *He looketh forth at the windows,*
> *Shewing himself through the lattice.*
> *My beloved spake, and said unto me,*
> *'Rise up, my love, my fair one, and come away.*

D'n Sept. 15, 45:

"How much I have to think of our Munich time and the *Englische Garten,* perhaps it was because we came to Munich in September. Through Francis the trees, the sky, the moon, the stars, became alive to me. We shared a great secret with them: 'When I consider thy heavens the work of thy fingers, the moon and the stars, which thou hast ordained O Lord, our Lord, how excellent is thy name in all the earth.' (8) "

D'n Sept. 19, 45:

"Yesterday helped Frau F. reaping the maize and then digging potatoes. We were the whole afternoon in the field and I was glad of the work, it helped me to get rid of my depression. How I would love to have our own little field. How we would enjoy the sowing and reaping. Last year in Wolfratshausen we had such beautiful Autumn days. On Monday night I looked at the sky. The constellation of the 'Bear' is now a bit different from Munich. How we loved the starry nights on the way to the *Chinesische* Restaurant. When will we look at them again together? There is only one thing that concerns me day and night and which makes me sad like "Ruth" in the alien corn-field. Had to think of her yesterday when reaping the maize:

> *the sad heart of Ruth, when, sick for home*
> *she stood in tears amid the alien corn;*
>
> ("Ode to a Nightingale" by Keats)

Have in a glass of water some beautiful yew-tree branches with red berries on them and a white flower, similar to a Christmas rose or waterlilies, only smaller. Do you remember these trees in the library garden of Luxemburg? How many things you made me love.

We shall also harvest apples and pears, in a different part of town. The fields are outside of Dornbirn, quite close to the Swiss border and the singular Säntis mountain, which we saw from your attic window on many an evening. The peace we got then from them, the stillness we had. When we said the psalm:

> *I will lift up mine eyes unto the hills,*
> *From whence cometh my help.*
>
> (Psalm 121)

D'n Sept. 20th, 45:
"My God — what a most precious day: at last a letter from Tiger! I don't want to go to bed to end this unique day. Everything now seems to me beautiful! And it so happened that I had made a cake, so we all, myself and the Fusseneggers, could celebrate together. We even had a bit of real coffee to go with it. And Luvah-Heart is all right — what a blessing — my God I thank you from all my heart — I can't write more — I am just too happy — 'whom my soul loves'. "

D'n Sept. 24th, 45:
"I have been helping Frau F a lot: peeling apples, bringing in pears etc. Spent a fine evening undisturbed in my little cave. Prayed a bit, then did some darning. It is very cold, snow has fallen on the mountains, our precious Mount Hermon. How lovely my little room is so far away from the world. If I could only conjure up Francis — when will I only see him again?

Yesterday I read Emily Brontë. She died at thirty — but how advanced she was as a mystic. In her all-consuming love she reminds me of Ste. Thérèse of Lisieux. What suffering she had to go through! Gave up the private Latin lessons. I found them boring — there is no fulfilment in that. Why not read poems, books or just do nothing and meditate. These few weeks here are given to me with a special purpose never again in my life will I have such leisure, such solitude."

D'n Oct. 11th, 45:
"Today I spent the whole day at the lake. How beautiful it is there, especially towards the evening. I could sit there day and night and do nothing else and just absorb all this beauty: the pale blue water with the white seagulls above it and the mountains with their coppery-coloured trees reflected in the water. It is all so simple and so miraculous. How Francis would have loved sitting here at the shores of Lake Constance."

D'n Oct. 16th, 45:
"I pray as before but now God gives me the feeling of being heard; I begin to feel his grace and feel especially that I am in his hands. I am so convinced that we should have trust. Yes, these were bright days for my soul where God gave me a bit of understanding. I must always think of the psalm: 'The Lord hath done great things for them' (26). How

miserable would I now be without Tiger, had we not in the last moment turned to God, what a blessing; otherwise I could not bear this separation. Now I know that Tiger and I are in our Truth one, and that we will be one together in our Truth. For us a life in Truth is only possible — nothing else.

How glad would I be for a letter, how I long for it. But that would be too much happiness. I am otherwise so well cared for.

Tiger-Heart, 'Whom my soul loveth'.

On November 8th at a quarter to nine in the evening I was upstairs alone in the warm kitchen, waiting for the return of the two women who went to the station each evening expecting some soldiers home. Suddenly there was a mad ringing of the front door and a few seconds later Frl Fussenegger appeared at the kitchen door holding Francis' little attaché case — which he had had with him since we left Berlin — triumphantly in her hands. A pang went through me and I don't remember how I reached the bottom of the stairs where Francis stood, I only knew that I was in his arms. Very touchingly the two women had thought that the immediate sight of Francis would be too much for me, so his attaché case was to prepare me for him.

When we were finally able to speak Francis told me about his desperate efforts to get back to Dornbirn. When he reached Paris his idea was first to get me to join him there and then for us to go to Ireland. But he discovered that it was impossible for us both to go there for the present. He therefore tried to return to Dornbirn, which proved to be extremely difficult, as it was very rare for anyone to travel eastward. But there were Yugoslavian partisans who naturally wanted to get home and Francis joined them. The major difficulty consisted in getting the correct documents to cross the border. He was sent to a camp in Metz, and from there to Strasburg where he got some kind of papers, but when he tried to cross the Rhine bridge he was stopped halfway by the French guards, who found the documents unsatisfactory and he was forced to return to Paris and start the whole business again. The French are sticklers for red tape, as I was to find out myself later. The only good thing was that Francis had good food, with plenty of white bread and red wine noodles in tomato sauce.

The second time he arrived in Strasburg with different documents and boarded a train with the Yugoslavian partisans which crossed the Rhine bridge without any interference by the French soldiers. Francis got off the train when it stopped on a sideline in German territory and said farewell to his Yugoslavian friends. This was in *Appenweiler*. He made for the next small *Gasthaus* (inn) which looked a bit dilapidated from the war, but to his joy and amazement he heard somebody playing one of Beethoven's piano sonatas. He felt he was at home, stayed the night there and took the express the next day to Dornbirn where he arrived in the evening. The Yugoslavian partisans had fought against Hitler and been put in camps by him, were freed by the Allies and sent home.

Francis' diary, November 10th:
"Ah, the great, great relief, the peace, the fulfilment of being back again with S. Last night we talked the whole night till five this morning. Today all is becoming calmer and I begin to see and taste the fruit of those three months of anguish."

Francis' diary, November 19th:
"There is the cold and the beginning of hunger again and the outer uncertainty.

We go to Mass at a quarter past seven, have breakfast of unsweetened black coffeee and a couple of slices of bread and cheese at eight. Afterwards I write for a couple of hours or so up in the kitchen, it is too cold in S's room. Lunch at twelve, mostly potatoes. In the afternoon we must cover ourselves in the bed because of the intense cold, practically four degrees of frost. Towards evening we do a bit of shopping and when it is dark or before we say our vesper prayers as always. Then supper, at present of some kind of coarse *Musmehl* flavoured with cocoa powder and coffee and two or three slices of bread and Wurst or bread and cheese. In the evenings we sit up in the kitchen for the sake of the warmth and sometimes play cards with Frl F.

Fine, fulfilled days, not lacking in hardship."

D'n Nov. 21st, 45:
"We have fine quiet days. Francis is upstairs and writing. How glad I am that he can write again. For the present we are left in peace and have enough to eat. We make our small bargains

70

in the shop, exchange cigarettes, that Francis brought from Paris, for *Musmehl*."

On the morning of the 21st of November Francis wrote in his diary: "Destiny leads us to more and more life in strange unknown ways." At half past four that afternoon there was a harsh ringing on the doorbell which practically never rang for us. It was dark outside already and I had just come in, after running home from my French lesson to start preparing for my birthday in two days time. Two plain-clothes French policemen came into the room and asked for a Gerda M. They began to search through all our belongings and grew very suspicious when they discovered some Swiss travel brochures. They told us to pack enough things for a few days and we were arrested and taken off to Bregenz prison.

Bregenz Prison Oberstadt:
These were frightful moments — up to this day I am anxious when opening the door to somebody unknown. Francis told me in the car that it looked bad for us. In Bregenz I was accused of having been a spy in Paris and Marseilles during the war, in 1941/42 under the name of Gerda M. Strangely enough, there did exist a Gerda M in Dornbirn because when I once fetched my ration cards, there was a mix-up with a Gertrude and Gerda M. My birth name is Gertrude. I could hardly believe all this and got the impression that the French were playing one of their charades with us and that they didn't believe all that stuff either, especially that Francis was to have been sympathetic to Hitler. But we never were officially charged. I wondered would the English have been behind this plot because of Francis' broadcasts to Ireland? But at least — while interrogated — we were not whipped or beaten up like other prisoners were. When we were brought to Bregenz Oberstadt prison — a huge dark building with tiny lit windows — I asked the warder, whether we could not stay together and he answered me: "Madame, you are not in a hotel here." No, and a hotel it certainly was not. Life was specially bad in those chaotic times after the war. Once in prison you could rot there till doomsday, there were no lawyers, no friends, nobody to help you from the outside. Food was the worst we ever tasted — we got boils all over our bodies, lice and fleas had a bumper time.

That's when I realised the value of the time I had spent in Dornbirn in prayer and meditation. So strangely enough I did not despair, but then at least Francis was under the same roof. I had some magic strength in me. I found in this painful process a most wonderful treasure. So far my main consolation had been the psalms, but now added to it was the Word of the Bible — often the only book we were allowed to have — which became to me something completely different from what I had seen in it so far. Passages which I had read before without making any imprint on me — their meaning just alluded me became suddenly alive, full of meaning and wonder. I just could not understand if I was really the same person who could have let these words of love, comfort and suffering slip through like a sieve?

But now I felt like what the psalmist says:

> *He brought me up out of a horrible pit and set my*
> *feet upon a rock.*

The Israelites reached their promised Land, Kanaa, the land of milk and honey and soon forgot their God over the worldly joys. While Moses, their spiritual leader, was only given a glimpse of it, from the top of the mountain, near the Promised Land, after which he died.

Luckily for me — my promised land lay not over in prosperous Switzerland. My soul would have rotted away there. I had to find that 'land' in *me,* as the prophet says:

> *He hath put a new song in my mouth;*
> *Yea, thy law, o Lord, is within my heart.*

(Psalm 40)

It was lucky for me also that I did it all on my own, that I had to go to prison to discover the word of Christ. I still belonged to that old school, who were not encouraged to read either the Old or the New Testament. We weren't encouraged to think about these matters. While in Dornbirn we did go to Mass, but it was in a Capuchin monastery or in the main church near us; but Mass was read by a very fine French chaplain, which made all the difference to us. Now you had to do things on your own, with only God's and Francis' help, as no one would come near the prison to bring us some spiritual comfort. It was not advisable to have anything to do with political prisoners, you could be tainted by them, or associated with them. What I learnt there was to rely on my own conscience, which I discovered I had, and had to take responsibility for it. These were all enormous discoveries for me, the importance of which only gradually sank into me and changed my views on many ways which I had taken for granted without questioning. I became critical of the world and its ways around me — that has stayed with me till today. Other things emerged which made an indelible impression on me and at the same time on Francis as well. Almost all the parables in the Bible which inspired us — nothing surpassed for me the beauty of the story of Mary Magdalene and Christ. We were overwhelmed by their relationship. She is the person who inspired me most and I would have loved to be her. Like her I could not imagine a life without love, no matter how imperfect that love is. Amongst all other women she is for me the morning and the evening star. Hers was a passionate nature, generous to the point of squandering herself who had no calculating soul, and was no hoarder of earthly riches. She possessed one treasure — a precious jar of ointment — and to the dismay of the disciples she poured it over His feet, after she had washed them with her tears of sorrow and wiped them with her long hair. She is called by many a sinner because of her various love-affairs. But why did she have them, not because she was superficial and flitted like a butterfly from one amusement to another. The contrary is true: her nature was so deep and passionate that nothing could fulfil her until she met the Lord; and then she virtually fell head over heels in love with Him. At last she had found Him whom her soul had been seeking, no one had ever called her 'Mary' so tenderly as our Lord after his resurrection.

To have discovered such treasures it was certainly worthwhile having spent some months in prison.

I had often to think of the heroine in Tolstoy's novel 'Resurrection' Katusha Maslova. In the course of the story she is brought before a court for having stolen a ring from a rich man. She is sentenced to Siberia, although being innocent. There she was: Katusha Maslova with her slight squint, and small energetic hands, in high boots, short fur cloak and headscarf ready for the long march to the final destination Siberia. Fifteen to twenty miles each day with one day's rest after two of marching. What terror this simple country-girl must have felt when she heard the sentence of being banished to Siberia with a gang of criminals. Yet, when the dreaded morning arrived — and she like the rest was being herded up like cattle — something extraordinary happened to her. Instead of the despair and hopelessness that Katusha had foreseen for herself, she suddenly saw that what was happening to her, far from being a disaster, was in a mysterious way bringing her closer to the God in whom she had always believed and also to her fellow beings. Out of this new insight she said to her companion on the long march: "There now, and I cried when I was sentenced. Instead of thanking God for it all the days of my life."

I know we were both yearning to be free, and together, which was only natural, but we were at least under one roof, and could exchange secret notes through our favourite warder Pappa Moser. He in fact was not a prison warder, had been in the border police, and was only now drafted in because of the shortage of staff and the overcrowded prison. Pappa Moser would often let me have a peep through the Judas hole in Francis' cell and I could see his face and send some greetings to him.

On Christmas Eve the French governor — looking like a spruce fighting-cock — took his prison chérie to celebrate Christmas with him somewhere in town. Our Austrian governor Herr Wiedl, whom we called 'Pluto', the hell's dog (Höllenhund) because of his devilish, always barking, nature also kept a low profile as he was spending the evening with his family. They lived in one wing of the prison. Most warders were on leave — and Pappa Moser was on duty in our wing. So when the coast was clear he brought Francis and another prisoner with whose wife I shared the cell to us. What a surprise! what unearthly joy! There had never been a better Christmas present than on that evening in Bregenz Oberstadt prison. Pappa Moser kept watch outside. We didn't know how long we stayed together. There was no time for counting the minutes, or half hours. We were happy beyond happiness.

All these moments made prison life endurable, especially when after Christmas I got a cell overlooking the exercise yard. Every morning I would climb to the iron-barred window and watch Francis going round and round in the yard. He knew I was up there — perched like a bird — but didn't dare give any sign or wave a hand. But what a comfort those moments were. They made the whole day brighter.

Sometime in the New Year the French, Belgian political prisoners, the so-called collaborators, were taken in weekly batches to their native country. These transports were dreaded, as it meant in most cases death for treason or collaboration. On March 12th, 1946, I smuggled a note to Francis telling him that I had heard that he would be transported in a few days with the French and Belgian prisoners to France, but that before any transport we would be allowed to say farewell. Here we had definitely touched rock-bottom very hard and there seemed to be no prospect of soaring up again. I was alone at that time in my cell and there was no comfort for me. Days and nights were an agony, which all the crying didn't help. I was completely forsaken. But one transport after another went without Francis being taken and the whole affair — the longer it took — fizzled out. Soon all the political prisoners had been transported to their fateful destiny.

Shortly before Easter I was taken for my second interview within five months. Suddenly everyone seemed pleasant, the whole atmosphere of suspicion had cleared. The fact was — although they did not admit it — there was no more suspicion against us. The subject didn't even come up. And the whole upshot of this sudden interview was that we were going to be free! So after all I had hit rock-bottom to come not only soaring up, but floating high in the clouds. Yet it took quite a few weeks before we finally left Bregenz Oberstadt Prison and then we were not actually free, although we thought that we were. On May 24th we boarded the train with two French officers. We thought they would just see that we got across the border into Germany, but no, they stayed with us, and we got off in Freiburg/Breisgau and were brought to Beethovenstr. and put in a cellar there. The German guard wanted to give us separate cellars, but the French, being more human told him: "Non, non, ensemble" (let them be together). At least we were together, even if not free. And the French (Freiburg was in the French occupied zone) treated us very decently. They were in fact quite sympathetic. We could stroll in the garden of the villa without a supervisor as long as we liked. Food was better

75

too. I passed the time standing at the cellar window watching the shoes of the passers-by. That's all I saw of them. We guessed what shoes might fit what person, and wondered would we ever see the person matching the shoes. And did they know how lucky they were to just walk along an ordinary street. These ordinary things became very precious to us. After four weeks in this cellar we were brought to the cellar next door and also told that soon we were to go free. Yet someone seemed to be playing cat-and-mouse with us. In the end it came out that we were to be transported to the English zone — the French having nothing against us, but the English apparently had something against Francis whose country had been neutral during the war. I daresay the English wanted to give Francis a lesson for having broadcast to Ireland during the war. The strain of the last weeks and the prospect of falling into the English hands — 'vae victis' — was too much for our inner reserve. Whatever was left there crumbled away — we felt completely forsaken by God, there was no longer even a prayer like "My God, my God, why hast Thou forsaken me?" Our hearts became embittered like stone.

But after only three days of that inner darkness — lo and behold — on July 13th, the day before the French national holiday, the day of the Bastille, we were simply told to pack our few belongings — as we were free, really, really free! So after eight and a half months imprisonment the gates were opened and Francis and I set free.

It was a glorious hot summer day. We were not used to that after the cold damp cellars, our pallor was that of mushrooms, we didn't feel too strong on our legs. But in spite of all that we straightaway took a walk through a meadow with our hearts overflowing with joy:

> *When the Lord turned again the captivity of Zion,*
> *We were like them that dream,*
> *Then was our mouth filled with laughter*
> *And our tongue with singing.*
> *The Lord has done great things for them.*

(Psalm 126)

Freiburg
August 10th, 1946:
And now we were free and each day was a miracle for us! We had a

small room, with flowers in a vase and our old pictures on the walls from Berlin and Dornbirn. Later we got a bigger room that the French had requisitioned. Flats or house-owners didn't like it but couldn't do anything about it. Germany had lost the war, and this was now the French occupied zone. All the different refugees from the East and displaced people ('DP') had to be housed, whether the locals like it or not. Our particular landlady in Schwarzwaldstr. no. 2 was not the nicest. There was a lot of quarrelling between her and her teenage daughter. I often thought that soon she would turn on me. I was allowed to cook towards evening at a certain time. But I felt very anxious. The Germans are such sticklers for cleanliness, polishing, scrubbing etc. When I think of Frau Fussenegger what an angel she was compared to our present, bedevilled lot. I had often found her sitting quietly in her kitchen reading the psalms or from her missal. Had she no other work to do: queuing up for food, cleaning, gossiping? When a nosy neighbour once asked her who we were she told them: "Go and ask them." She always had a wonderful smile, she was too simple to be able to explain things. Later, when I came on a psalm, which is still my favourite for everyday life, I thought it was applicable to her:

Except the Lord build the house, they labour in vain
that build it.
It is vain for you to rise up early, to sit up late, to eat
the bread of sorrow:
For so He giveth his beloved in sleep!

Life in Schwarzwaldstr. no. 2 was naturally less dramatic than in the previous months, except for two to three nights when Francis was again taken by the French securité to Beethovenstr. 7. But it wasn't really imprisonment. That French Alsatian officer was genuinely interested in Francis' life and motives and writing. They had all-day-long sessions. I could visit Francis and bring him anything I liked. But now I was very suspicious and sent off a telegram to Francis' publisher Gollancz — with the result that I was also put in the adjoining cellar — just to keep my mouth shut. The telegram naturally was intercepted and never reached Gollancz. But apart from that small incident the French left us in peace. Life for us was beautiful, we enjoyed all the smallest and most simple tasks, and didn't neglect our evening vespers. At last Francis was able to write again, and while he was writing I gave private English lessons to many of the refugees — Lithuanians, Estonians, Latvians, Hungarians, etc. who all wanted to emigrate to America, which was for them the land of milk and honey. Most of them had no knowledge of English. Through the lessons I met my dearest of friends, a Lithuanian woman called Jadwiga. Herself and her sister always insisted that Francis come to the lessons as, with the special skill they seemed to have on the black market, they always made these sessions into a little feast, with sandwiches and a drink. We needed the money from these lessons badly as the old German mark had been devalued. Whatever your savings were you only received forty new German Reichsmark. This was a hard blow for those who lived on their savings. Suddenly the shops were full of all kinds of goods, but people didn't dare buy them, as they were afraid to touch their forty marks.

The refugees of different nationalities managed to bring a bit of life into bourgeois Freiburg. The nicest group of them were the Lithuanians, who were an incredibly lively and zestful bunch of people. They gave parties the like of which I have never seen before, which usually lasted for three or four days, until somebody really collapsed. The tables would be laden with all kinds of food and the drink would be constantly flowing. I never discovered where they got everything from, but as I said they were great dealers on the black market, and their generosity was boundless.

If life in freedom was a miracle never to be forgotten — we still had our hardships. Food was short, apart from these rare occasions, especially after the war. We were constantly hungry. The Freiburgers were better off, naturally, they would mostly have some connections with the hinterland. The same applied to the fuel situation. We also got some trees in the Black Forest to fell. But how could we? We had no axe, no cart and no strength to fell a tree at all. Francis was especially weak. And although we got a secondhand stove, a nice-looking old thing, so homely, we didn't dare to even ask to have any pipes put in for the smoke. The landlady would not have liked it. The winters were hard to bear. We spent most of the time in bed, in a kind of hibernation — until by chance we met Frau Piening who had a small flat with a stove and fuel. We met her through Nora, who had been a few days in prison in Beethovenstr. no. 1. She lived quite close to us and it was at her home that we met Frau P. She definitely was, as they say in Germany, a soul of a person, but she was not from Southern Germany, but came originally from Westphalia. She was outgoing and warmhearted and compassionate. She took us all under her wings, including several Rumanians amongst us. We would sit the whole afternoon round the tiled stove and sometimes she would dish up a hot thick potato soup. She became our mother, our "Mutti". So we trudged in all weathers to Mutti, who lived with her daughter on the other side of Freiburg. We had to cross the market square, completely destroyed in the air-raids. The cathedral in its centre alone had miraculously escaped. Freiburg in general was badly damaged during the attacks, and like in Berlin and Munich and other cities, you just had vast vistas of rubble where once streets and rows of houses stood.

Apart from Mutti, who was such a help to many of us, there were the Quakers who had moved into barracks opposite the University as soon as the war ended. They were mainly there to help the students with books and warm rooms and some hot meals. Betty Collins ran the place. Seeing them in their work one couldn't help but be reminded of the good Samaritan in the bible. Francis was glad when he discovered the library with so many books. He gave some talks there for the students. I remember especially one on Auden. Then there was Jerry, an ex-American soldier, who worked with the Quakers. He was a very good person. He would do his best to get us out — to France if possible — but if all failed, he would marry me — like Frank Ryan long ago. But he didn't have to — through his help we got a family later in Paris who vouched for me.

It was in early February 1947, which was bitterly cold, when we were so hungry, that food became such an obsession that even in our dreams we were not free from them. Mountains of food stuff lay there only waiting to be eaten — but at those very moments we would wake up. Someone had sent money, I think from Ireland, for a food parcel through Caritas, a Catholic organisation whose aim was and very likely still is, to help the poor and hungry. It was going when I was a child, and I remember Mother belonging to it. Caritas, as is implicit in its name, means love, care. Our Caritas in Freiburg got the food parcels from nearby Switzerland. It is only a crow's flight away. This transaction went much quicker than the normal post parcels or later the care parcels which often took months. But they always arrived! Anyhow, knowing that our first, precious food parcel was in the Caritas building, we plucked up all our courage and went there. We dreaded these public places having experienced in them so much disappointment and down-right nastiness. The people working in the Caritas building — so well-fed, probably from the food-parcels — with their indifferent airs — were repugnant to us. They would prevaricate with us, firstly telling us there was no parcel, then they sent out a notification that there was a parcel after all. And if we hadn't got it yet, it was very likely still in the main sorting office of the post-office, and if not there we would definitely get it the following morning. We did go to the post-office, and the officials looked everywhere, but found nothing. We didn't believe a word of all that tripe — it was sheer nastiness to keep the parcel from us as long as possible. Very likely it gave them a sadistic joy. Of course, nothing came with the morning post. We spent a terrible evening with three slices of dried bread, and went fully dressed to bed because it was so cold. We went to Mutti the following day, soon after lunch (although we had, of course, no lunch) and told her of our plight. Mutti said nothing, put on her coat, took us with her, and with a very set determined face, made straight for the Caritas. She would have nothing of that sly mealy-mouthed way, she was forthright, honest and her goodness did not mean weakness. She stood her ground there and thundered like a tigress when politeness didn't work, and she would not budge an inch — the parcel was there — they themselves had acknowledged it — even if not by post — the slip for it was there after all so it did not belong to them, but to Mr Stuart. In the end our Mutti won, Francis was given the precious gift and had to sign that wretched slip, which had never been sent. Imagine our joy — we practically floated home on clouds to Mutti's place, where she first made a good cup of coffee with plenty of sugar and powdered milk. After that we opened one of the delicious tins of meat and lard and butter. Mutti made a meal of it. After that repast Francis felt strong enough to help Mutti chop the logs in the yard. He swung the axe like a Goliath and we all had to laugh. I carried the wood upstairs and piled it up in the balcony, while Mutti busied herself with the evening meal in the kitchen, to which we had invited a couple of hungry Bulgarians. After a while Francis and I rested for a moment on a log in the first warm shafts of spring sunlight. Spring seemed to be in the air and to fill our cup of bliss, we saw the first snowdrops in a corner of the yard. Yes, we felt, He did look after us in a miraculous way. When the need was greatest He stepped in: "He that keepeth thee will not slumber" and showered us with spiritual and earthly blessings, but you had to have 'Geduld'.

> *Neither reckon, nor calculate,*
> *but ripen like a tree that trusts the*
> *Spring storms without anxiety that there will be no*
> *Summer. It will follow for certain, but only for the*
> *patient ...*
> *This I learn daily, painfully and am grateful:*
> *Patience is everything.*
> (Rilke: from 'Briefe an einen jungen Dichter')

That incident with the Caritas left a bitter taste in me and since then I distrust any so-called do-gooders rattling their tins in the streets or at the door.

Again there followed for us desperate times of hunger. But we believed that we would be saved from starvation, not through our own efforts or through those of others sending us parcels, but through God's grace in His own time. When we had again reached the peak of hunger another of those miracles happened. Totally unexpectedly we were invited by the wife of a French officer to supper one Friday night. And what a feast of a meal it turned out to be. Francis described it in his diary:

"What a supper we had on Friday night at Mme A's. I think I have never sat down with such hunger to such a meal. First came tapioca soup, which we ate sweet by adding some sugar. At the same time, not being sure of what would follow, I began to eat the huge slices of white bread that Mme. A. had piled in a bread basket as quickly and unostentatiously as possible. Next came pork and cauliflower, which we both had two helpings of. Then, having heard from S. about our desperate position, Mme. A. ran out to the kitchen and heated up a dish of *"Nudeln"* and meat that was over from lunch. After this came cake, from which we each ate a huge slice and a kind of custard pudding. Nor were we short of white wine which we drank steadily all the time. Then Mme A. brought in cheese and I ate another slice of bread — my fourth — with it. Finally we drank a large cup of very strong coffee laced with brandy. It was such a meal that I had not even dared to dream of, much less eat, since I don't know when. Even the rare good meals that we have come by now and then, were nothing like this."

Soon after our first parcel on the 3rd February we received another one containing five pounds of fat. The first parcel was all gone, but now we had fat to fry our bread in. So we were living in some comfort for a while, were able to buy a little coffee on the black market, and, for breakfast had café au lait with the rich powdered milk, with sugar in it and fried bread and bacon.

On March 5th when we were again very low I made up my mind to go to the *'Wirtschaftsamt'* with Francis' passport to apply on his behalf as an Irishman for the Irish bacon that was being distributed to the sick and the old. Francis anyhow was so weak with malnutrition that I kept him in bed. I had little hope but I was desperate. And it was not long before I returned to Francis with a pound of bacon fat and several pounds of potatoes in my arms. I had been refused at the *'Badishes Hilfswerk'* by the first official. I pleaded and became so overwrought that I burst into tears when they didn't give me anything. Then a girl secretary had pity on me and took me to a higher official who was very sympathetic and gave me the necessary slip with which to buy the bacon at our butcher's. Then on the way back I called on George, the French soldier, whose wife had given us that gorgeous meal — and asked him for a few potatoes. I got a few pounds. But on the whole way I had prayed and prayed — and there another sweet little miracle had happened. I read to Francis from my missal the passage of the flour and the oil which never diminished.

82

On March 21st, after again enduring endless hunger, we were literally showered with food-parcels: four arrived from Switzerland and a notification from the *Sparkasse* (saving bank) that there was a care-parcel for us. Those care-parcels coming from America were something quite out of this world. They weighed forty to fifty pounds and contained nearly everything possible to eat: wonderful real coffee, powdered milk, sugar, fat, tins of meat, chocolate, cigarettes etc. We could hardly bear so much earthly joy! We had been reduced again to dry bread and had in fact had nothing for breakfast. There were at the moment many parcels on the way from England, Ireland and America. Being sent in January or February they arrived now.

One of those people who helped us and others most was Ethel Mannin and her husband Reginald, who was a Quaker. They spent their weekends just making up parcels. You could send up to seven pounds at a time. And on Saturday, June 21st, she arrived in Freiburg in a green chauffeur-driven car with the Union Jack flying on its bonnet. The front door must have been open (it was usually locked) as there was a knock at our door and she just walked in! We had given up hope of seeing her. It meant a great deal to Francis, as she had been a close friend of his. But there she was! We all went down and met Mac, her driver, a very cheerful fellow and carried the goodies up. People in the street stared at the English car, we were for a few minutes *the* event in the district. Ethel had managed to come as a correspondent for an English paper. She was coming from Vienna where she had visited some poor hungry people. We feasted from the delicious tins and drank Chianti wine. When she left on Monday at about 9.30 we were heartbroken. When we said goodbye as the car moved on, and we returned to our empty room, we just sat down and cried. We were so nervously exhausted from all the excitement, that we lay down and went to sleep.

About a year later Ethel came again, this time by train. She saw to it that we didn't go too long without any parcels. Any friend of hers had to help, and give parcels to Europe instead of presents at Christmas. So when it came to Christmas 1948 we had three care-parcels.

On the day after Christmas I sat with Francis beside me on the couch, writing in my diary, and thought back about the

Francis leaving Dornbirn for the last time, August 1945

With Francis' children, Ian and Kay Stuart, Freiburg, 1948

With Ethel Marrim in their room, Freiburg, 1947

happy events in the year that had just passed. My sister with her Martin from Berlin had visited us, and then Ethel Mannin had come to stay again, this time without car and driver, and had spent practically a whole week in our company. When she left we were much calmer and the future seemed brighter. I received the status of a displaced person, having been born in Danzig, which was now part of Poland. In practical terms this meant that emigration was now possible for me.

The most important news however was that although we only had one room which was piping hot in summer and freezing in winter, Francis had begun to write again, and I typed it at Mutti's who had a typewriter. And then Victor Gollancz accepted two of his novels, *The Pillar of Cloud,* which was loosely based on our experiences in Freiburg, and *Redemption.* This was an immense joy to us and Gollancz was so enthusiastic that he even sent the most wonderful telegram which we could hardly grasp. We were overwhlelmed, especially when we considered that Gollancz was a Jew who could have resented Francis' stay in Germany during the war. *The Pillar of Cloud* was published in 1948, with a second edition later that year, and a third edition in 1949. On the cover of the book Compton Mackenzie wrote: "Wonderful: the most profound book about the aftermath of the war I have read in any language. I really am left without words to express my admiration."

The manuscripts were sent through Betty Collins of the Quakers, who had better communication with England, as the post was still not really functioning. In May 1949 *Redemption* was published, which Victor Gollancz printed on the cover as "Francis Stuart's Redemption", and Compton MacKenzie added: "I think *Redemption* is a magnificent book, and if its beauty and terror do not win Francis Stuart the recognition he deserves I shall begin to despair of contemporary English criticism."

Although the books enjoyed such success we did not benefit from it as yet, as it was impossible to get any royalties from them in Freiburg. Many years later we were to experience a similar joy in Ireland when Francis' novel *Black List: Section H,* was enthusiastically accepted by Professor Harry T. Moore of the Southern Illinois University Press. I wrote in my diary in April 1970: "The best news of all is that Francis' book has been taken. We got the good news in a telegram after the rejection from Michael Gill here in Ireland just two days ago with a comment from him 'that as a novel the book does not start to exist.' Very depressing news and that after years of rejection also in England where Francis was really *blacklisted.*"

We had an especially beautiful Christmas again that year, 1948, with care-parcels. Nurse Dinger, in the next room, had offered us her warm room as she had a stove in it and she was away with friends in the country. So we left the door between them open and felt warm and cosy in our own room at last. We spent those days in bliss as if in another world. And on that Silvester Eve we drank to a change in 1949 that might see us perhaps in Venezuela, England or France?

On the 29th June, 1949, we were still in Freiburg and met our friends from America, Ricky and Mary Austin, in the German part of the station at Basle. We spent the whole afternoon with them. They were laden down with gifts for us that were so heavy that they had to be sent on by post later. And as we missed our train back we had to walk to the next station through the night. It was a beautiful walk. We went along a stream through meadows and were enchanted by the landscape. We passed a small cottage with a stork's nest on the roof and a sleeping stork standing on one leg in it. The sickle of the new moon rose above the stork's bent head and all around us millions of glittering glow worms danced. It was to be our last walk together in Germany, especially precious to us because on the evening of July 2nd, Francis left for Paris. Jerry, the American Quaker, was already there and he was hopeful of getting a family to vouch for me, but Francis would have to do all the running around to get the different papers necessary for my entry into France. Before leaving we had found a smaller room for me with a separate entrance and a water tap on the landing, that seemed ideal. Francis would not have been able to rest easy thinking of me stranded in that big room with the unpleasant landlady in Schwarzwaldstr no 2.

It was an incredibly hot summer when the walls of the houses absorbed the heat and then blasted it back so that you felt you were in an oven. If possible, people only ventured out towards evening or early in the morning. I spent most days in the new modern swimming pool outside Freiburg with a friend, or lay on the bed of my small cosy room, reading and rereading

Francis' letters. Francis had hope that, if I only had *'patience'* he would manage to get me over. As he later told me, Paris was equally hot and tramping from one office to the next was totally exhausting. But Jerry introduced him to the Dormandis, a Hungarian-Jewish family, who had left Hungary in the mid-thirties to escape from the threatening Hitler regime. They lived in Avenue de Breteuil and soon offered Francis a *'mansarde'* (garret) on the top floor as his hotel became too expensive. They would also vouch for me, as long as Francis took care of the papers. I could only enter the country as a domestic, and although they didn't need me, (having a *Mme de chambre*) their friend opposite would be glad to have me, as domestics were very difficult to get. The news seemed unbelievable to me when in August I received the special *'laisser passer* (letter of passage?). At once I packed all my belongings in a large wooden box and made for the screening camp in Rastatt. It was the dream of every refugee to get to Paris, but very few ever got the chance. But once again fortune had swung my way and on August 19th, I arrived in Meau near Paris.

Chapter Three

PARIS

After having been screened once again — I don't know how often in all — and found to be okay I heard the telephone ringing: *"Allô, allô, M. Dormandi, votre domestique est arriveé. Voulez-vous la chercher de la Gare de l'Est, Merci."* Heavenly words to my ear. And there Francis met me with a bunch of white carnations. It was all like a dream and I thought, of all things, about Noah and his animals — when they could finally open the gates and man and beast stepped on the earth, into a new beautiful world — like paradise. That's how I felt at that very moment. After all the sadness — what a joy — after all the endless and endless *'Geduld'* — what a reward. Even the metro welcomed me with *'Bienvenue'*. I was received by everyone like the prodigal daughter with flowers and one sweet little instant sticks in my mind. When Francis and I arrived in Dormandi's flat and went into Laci's study, he offered me a seat in one of the deep leather armchairs and in his quiet, shy, but always correct way, offered me a Camel cigarette (which reminded me of the care-parcels) with a piece of bitter chocolate. As I sat there, an exhausted and overwrought stranger surrounded by such unimaginable luxury, his gesture made me feel completely at home. From that moment I loved him.

But Francis had something in store for me which was hard to equal. He hadn't forgotten how much I had taken to the Siamese cat with the French couple in Lindau waitingroom on our flight, and how I had often wondered what could have happened to it in that chaos. A few days before my arrival Francis had been sitting on a couch in Dormandi's flat, when one of the kittens playing with the others, had stalked over to him, settled in his lap and fell asleep there — completely at ease

— it had chosen its master and home. Francis knew how delighted I would be with it. So I had to close my eyes, cup my hands and then he put something soft, furry and purring into them. It was Mlle. Sophie, who became the *'objet de notre tendresse.'*

The Dormandis, Ricky and Mary, Austin and Francis' publisher, M. Lesort, really spoilt us. We went out a lot and stayed in M. Lesort's villa in Versailles for a time when he was on holidays. But the luncheon on Sept. 14th which Victor Gollancz gave in our honour was something unique. His wife, daughter and other, quite distinguished people, were there. It was all a bit confusing to me as I didn't know anyone. But V.G. took me under his wing, insisting that I sit next to him — and I felt fine. We drank quite a lot and had delicious food and a most exotic dessert which I didn't know, but V.G. again insisted that I would like it. So I did. It was *zabaglione*. Then when we parted V.G. took my hand and kissed it in front of the whole crowd! What an honour!

Sept. 28th, 1949:
"We got another little attic room on the landing in the passage from the Dormandis. It needs painting and cleaning. It has an open fireplace, just the thing for the coming winter. Then Francis got a writing-desk from the Dormandis, chairs, bookcase etc. What wonderful people they are. They make up for all the unpleasant landladies in Munich, Tuttlingen and Freiburg. We feel very happy and at peace."

Paris, Nov. 24th, 49:
"Yesterday was my birthday. Francis got up early, cleaned the room and made breakfast. I had to stay in bed. Then he brought in the breakfast tray with two burning candles, a little cake and pressed something into my hand out of his trouser pocket — a note book. It touched me very much. After lunch we went to the Louvre, then had a quiet tea at home and in the evening came the crown of the day, how nice that it had to be my birthday. His publisher gave a reception for Francis:

"Les Editions de Temps Présent vous prient de bien vouloir honorer de votre présence la réception qu'elles donneront en l'honneur de M. Francis Stuart, le mercredi

89

*23 Novembre 1949 de 18 a 20 heures, chez Madame
Sauvageot, 59, rue de Babylone, Paris 7."*

What an evening! what a grand day in Paris! The old saying
come to mind, it is actually in St. Matt. (13.57): "A prophet
is not without honour, save in his own country and in his own
house."

February 25th, 50 (Francis' diary):
"Yesterday S. had the operation for appendicitis at ten in the
morning, and I went to the hospital at half past one and she
saw me coming as soon as I got to the top of the stairs through
the open door and weakly raised her bare arm. (Once I remember in prison in the early hours how she thrust in her arms
through the little *aperture* (Judas) in the door and beckon me
from my bunk). Am alone here with Sophie."

February, 28th, 50 (Francis' diary):
"Visiting S. from 1.30 to 2.30 or 3 every day. Those are fine
moments, quiet, peaceful and tender. She is getting on all
right although this morning had some fever again."

March 29th, (Francis' diary):
"Dinner with Liam O'Flaherty and Kitty on Saturday and an
evening at The Flore and the Dôme. A strange meeting again
aften ten years. Much laughter and talk of old times and friends,
but some echo of sadness beneath it. He told me that he and
Kitty were no longer living together. They were to lunch
yesterday and left for London in the evening, Liam en route
for Aran and Kitty for America."

What we enjoyed most in Paris were the Sunday afternoon
races at Longchamp. We walked from the metro station through
to Bois de Boulogne. That was really a first-class meeting, with
first-class jockeys and around the 6th of June or so we were at
Chantilly to see the French Derby. There was great excitement
with a close finish between Tentième and Scratch. Francis was
shouting his head off, the sweat was pouring down his face, he
swore that Tentième had won. It was a hotly disputed decision
(there was no photo-finish camera) which the French love forever discussing. Anyhow Scratch was given the race and
Tantième's jockey made some not too flattering remarks when

passing the stewards. But next time the two animals met there was no photo-finish and Tantième beat Scratch easily. That's racing for you.

On June 29th Liam O' Flaherty turned up. We had a simple lunch of potatoes and butter with no wine. We were always short of money. But Liam enjoyed the "spuds" and loved to drink water from the tap in the passage. It is actually the only time that I saw him eating properly and enjoying it. He would usually order the biggest steaks and meals and leave them practically untouched (nice tit-bit for Mlle Sophie). Needless to say there had to be at such occasions several bottles of red wine on the table. Liam would never order one bottle and another later. He had to have all in front of him. We often found it very hard to get through the lot. But at that little luncheon in our attic overlooking Montmartre Liam shone in a rôle I had never before known him: the storyteller. It was as if he had opened a magic suitcase full of wonderous tales, credible or incredible, they were sheer magic. I was spellbound. Stories when he had won one or two pounds would end up with suitcases full of pound notes so that he even couldn't carry the lot and had to take a taxi and then put the whole lot on a hack and lose it all. He loved to lose, and would never bet on the obvious, the certainty in racing.

We went out a lot with Liam who now lived in a small hotel, not so smart as the 'Lutetia' where he stayed with Kitty when we first met them. One day we wanted to go racing to St. Cloud in early July but Liam was late and so he hailed a taxi which left us short of money. But didn't I find a thousand Franc note on the ground. There were so many Arabs there shuffling about in tennis-shoes with loads of money. We were delighted and instead of water drank wine. On the way home Liam, who was in front next to the driver while we sat at the back, entertained the whole bus by shouting, amongst other things, a joke in French and then in English: "Francis the wolves are howling." No one understood the actual meaning, but it was hilarious.

But that wasn't the only time I found a big Franc-note. Once afternoon leaving one of the summer parties of Gallimard, which were given for the writers whom they had published recently — with champagne and *petit fours* we ended up in the Café Flore with no money to spare when something brushed my leg — a black pussycat. I stooped to caress it and came up with a five-hundred Franc-note. Liam thought I had magic in me.

One afternoon I had promised Mme Casaliz for whom I worked in the mornings that I would help her that afternoon — but not for too long — preparing and laying the table for her women friends. Punctually — we had arranged to go out with Liam — there was a knock at the door and a well-dressed gentleman in a light grey suit with darker stripes asked for Mme Stuart in a most charming way in excellent French. The ladies at the table sipping coffee and eating *marron gateau* held their breath — Liam was so handsome. He took my arm and we went down the front stairs, I usually had to take the back-stairs meant for traders, and domestiques. *"Vraiment votre petite domestique a de la chance,"* is what they said after-wards. They craned their necks at the window and saw us driving off with Francis in the taxi. Liam in full anticipation of an evening in Montmartre shouted: "Whip up the horses, Andrej, and drive up with a dash." (Dimitri Karamazov on the drive to Mokroe). There and then I grasped fully the fairy story of Cinderella who eventually got her prince. I still see myself as that cinderella to whom all these miracles happened.

With Liam I shall always remember the song "Lili Marlene". When we were once watching the horses in a parade ring rhythmically stepping, Liam would suddenly say: "Look they step to the tune:

Un-ter-der-La ter-ne-vor-dem-ho-hen-Tor,
Staht eine Laterne und steht sie noch davor.
Dort wollen wir uns wiederseh'n,
bei der Laterne wollen wir stehn mit dir Lili Marlene,
mit dir Lili Marlene.

Later he would sing it in Irish. That song became our signal song whenever we would meet. Even a few months ago, in 1983, when I visited him with Kitty and his mind was in darkness so that he didn't recognise me — I sang softly to him *"Unter de Laterne, bei dem hohon Tor,"* and for a few seconds his face and eyes lit up and he even hummed a few bars with me. But then all became oblivion.

When I got my holidays we went to Denneville, but it was a

Liam O'Flaherty and Kitty, Paris, 1950

With Sophie, outside Paris, 1950

With Ricky Austin at Versailles, 1949

windy and desolate spot by the sea and the water was too icy for us; Francis wanted to go on to Deauville, but by then I was homesick for Sophie. So we returned home via Lisieux, where we stopped and looked around. It attracted us because it was the home town of St Thérèse. We visited her home and the convent chapel. Then over supper in a restaurant we started talking about the little saint who is a great favourite of ours. Many people today can't accept any longer the cult of complacent and sugary piety, that 'little, white flower', smiling sweetly down on us amidst a rain of rose-petals of sentimentality. It is a great pity she was ever presented to us with touched-up photos and her own autobiography was tampered with by her sister. 7,000 alterations were made in the manuscript in order to make her immediately popular. The climate has now changed — but great harm has been done.

It's true St Thérèse did not come from a very attractive background but from a very narrow-minded atmosphere. But she grew out of this conventional, pious religiousness and reached mature spirituality in Mount Carmel.

I am sure that had Thérèse been born in the gutter like the little singing sparrow of Paris, Edith Piaff, and that other woman of Bethany, Mary Magdalene (all three of whom were so full of love and passion), that she too would have taken to roaming the streets looking for somebody to fasten their love onto. I think it is very relevant, and not surprising, that the great chanson-singer always prayed to St. Thérèse before retiring at night. And none of these three women ever regretted their search for love with all the follies it entailed.

I will rise now and go about the city in the streets,
And in the broad way i will seek him whom my soul loveth.

After our supper in Lisieux we took a night train to Paris, back to Sophie and the small world we had built in our flat.

During the summer of 1950 we began to get uneasy again. The world situation looked very dark, war was raging in Korea and there was trouble in other countries. Once again, we were without a permanent home, and feared being deported or separated from each other. So Francis took the first tentative steps about finding a place to live and settle down. The only country that seemed to offer hope was South Africa and

Francis went to their Legation to make enquiries and got application forms for me. There seemed to be no major difficulties, in fact the major problem was getting together the fare for both of us (around £150) and having enough left over to start a life together. But, thankfully, we were not meant to go to South Africa. Firstly the money was not there and Francis' mother had a stroke and he had to go and visit her in Ireland. And even after she had recovered, we still didn't want to travel too far away from her.

In late Autumn of 1950 I began a new diary with the words: *"Tantième enlève brillament l'Arc de Triomphe 1950."* I am delighted to begin this notebook with the news of our wonderful racing outing to Longchamp, where Tantième beat Scratch, the Boussac horse, who had been the controversial Derby winner at Chantilly in the closest of close finishes, by more than four lengths. The weather was freezing and there was a downpour of rain. We could only go to the *pelouse*, being cheaper and had no shelter at all from the elements. But we had a good position at the rails and nothing could have shifted us from our vantage point. The rain had stopped at least for the main race. The horses came out parading and pirouetting: 'Un-ter-der-La-ter-ne', Tantième was in a sweat — but we had such faith in him as he had only once been beaten so far, and that was in the controversial Derby result. But he had to meet Scratch again — and then we would see! On this memorable Arc-Day Tantième had his revenge in great style. There was to be no photo-finish this time, that was sure. By God — we shouted him home with heart and soul — and he won so easily — nothing could have touched him, he glided past them all and left Scratch four lengths behind. Doyasbère, his jockey, in grey-silver casque and pink cap, was all smiles! Shivering with the cold and excitement, soaked through, we collected our money, had something warm to drink and returned home, again in pouring rain through the Bois de Boulogne to our little Sophie who was purring her heart out when she heard us coming.

With South Africa gone and Francis' mother in such bad health, Francis tried to get me into Ireland, but on the 2nd May, 1951, we heard that my application had been refused. It upset me deeply as I seemed to be a constant clog to Francis. But one more setback didn't matter much to us, as we had survived so many together. And then Ethel Mannin once again came to our rescue. She was willing to vouch for me as her domestic, even though she didn't need one. So in early June I got my visa for England and, if all went well, we would arrive there on the 17th of June. But it wasn't only myself that needed papers, Sophie would need them as well, and in addition would have to be placed in quarantine for six long months. That was a dreadful prospect for us. I was sad to be leaving "gay Paris," I thought then, and still do, that it was a wonderful city. Francis felt that we might return and live there again, but we never did. What I most regret about that leave-taking in retrospect was to leave behind many of our letters to each other in prison, as well as letters by Samuel Beckett and other friends of Francis to him during the war and some of Francis' manuscripts including the original text of *Redemption*. These were all later lost.

Chapter Four

LONDON

On Monday, June 18th, 1951, we arrived in London's Victoria Station. We left France at Dieppe and were three hours on board till Newhaven. It was a lovely, sunny day on the ship, and the seagulls followed us until we had nearly reached England. We saw the famous cliffs of Dover, all white with a band of green on top. I had to undergo a medical examination and another screening — I should have really counted how often I was screened — they must have thought that all refugees carried leprosy. But at last I stepped out of the booth with Francis anxiously waiting for me — would there be another hitch at the last moment? Was I being kept long inside? But I was free! Only Sophie had to be handed over to the carrying agent, she wasn't even allowed to leave the ship. Over the loudspeaker, while we were still on board, we heard our name called informing us that "Mr Stuart's cat" was not to leave the ship, she will be met by someone from the quarantine. What struck me later was that we could have easily smuggled her in a bag — but I had been too nervous at that time. Another time — I thought!

What struck me most when driving through England was the luscious green. Rilke would have said *"Grün wirklicher Grüne."* (green, real green) On the continent the grass was at that time always parched. Ethel met us at the station and we went to her place 'Oak Cottage' in Wimbledon. There were lots and lots of new impressions to take in: the endless rows of houses, all had fake columns at the front door and over it a kind of balcony. I found that sight a bit depressing.

But most important, at that moment, were the visits to Sophie in Hackbridge kennels. The moment she arrived we got a card that we could visit her any time and that it would do her good. They seemed at least to be concerned with her welfare. The first time we visited her she was in her outer compartment, but when the girl wanted to pick her up, she hissed at her, so Francis went round and picked her up and she climbed on his shoulder and purred and went on purring for most of the time we were there. Kennels in general are sad for animals and owners, but this kennel was really good. First each cat had two little rooms, really rather big, and not like here in Ireland, a single one not bigger than a telephone booth. There were plenty of shelves to jump on and ladders to climb, and then there was a window in the wall to get into the outer compartment. And this had all sorts of amusements for the animals: logs, stumps of trees for scratching and they were just surrounded by wire. The food was good: tinned salmon to begin with. And at the front door entrance was a shelf on which the cats mostly sat watching out for any visitor. When anyone entered they all started to miaow. There were cats from all over the world. Then when we left we had a very vivid impression of her fear or sadness. Her quick jumping down to the door, her eyes looking up anxiously, her crying and jumping up again to the shelf at the bars. We couldn't conceive of an expression of more affection than she showed at our visit. How strange this emotion of a small animal.

Whenever we came Sophie would recognise our voices and jump on the little shelf near the entrance door. We could stay as long as we liked, and could come at any time, and we were even allowed to take her out onto a big lawn (fenced in naturally). Gradually she gained confidence and would eat better and so got a bit stronger, although she never touched the titbits we brought her — but she ate them when we were gone. With us she just purred and was very excited as we played with her on the lawn.

We stayed for a while with Ethel, then visited some friends and finally returned to London, where I had to take up work as a domestic, as Ethel didn't need me. But it was not difficult to get cleaning work. That's why the refugees were allowed in, to do the dirty work that the English didn't want to do. I think I got 2/6 per hour. I had two jobs going and made £3 in a week. We were glad of it, as money was scarce but jobs were plentiful. Even Francis found easily an odd job here and there. One bedsitter followed another with a little gas ring for cooking. I

Madeleine on the boat to London, 1951

At Oak Cottage, Wimbledon, 1951

Francis and Ethel, Oak Cottage, 1951

think we got to know all the corners of Earls' Court. During a speech on the occasion of F's eightieth birthday recently Anthony Cronin applied the following passage to our first acquisition of a room of our own after moving to London from Paris in this apt and touching description of fragile security:

> *The shutter just hasped, the storm shut out, the*
> *quarrel forgotten, the love flow,*
> *As in a furnished room*
> *With the saucepan on the gas ring*
> *And the bus fare for tomorrow*
> *Though only the books from the library*
> *And the landlord across the hall*
> *Between two trusting people*
> *A satisfaction of sense*
> *A bright circle of time*
> *A little republic of love.*

('Reductionist Poem' by Anthony Cronin,
published by Raven Arts, Dublin)

Shortly before Christmas we took a proper flat in 30a Collingham Gardens for the sake of Sophie. She was due out on December 18th, 51. It was simply wonderful having her back — although we could hardly afford the rent, and on top of that pets were not allowed. But our place was an annex and the landlady who lived in the main building never came near us, thanks be to God. Sophie took the rough coconut carpet for a scratching board and it looked soon like a stubble field. I had to put the ends sticking out back every day. We managed it there for nine months, Francis took up some nightwork as a security man and did some translating. I did not like London but thankfully we were never too far from Hyde Park or Holland Park to take a stroll in the evening.

On the 27th May, 1952, Francis and I started for Epsom for our first English Derby. (Francis had been to the Derby in previous years, before the war). Weeks before we were already deeply involved in studying the form of the horses. 'Tulyar' was our main hope. Francis took a fancy to it the year before, when we saw it running as a two-year-old. Then he won at Hurst Park as a three-year-old, where Francis and Liam saw

100

him and both came home completely enthusiastic about his Derby chances. We took the train to Epsom — my wish since I knew Francis and I had heard so much about it had been to see Epsom on Derby day. We reached Tattenham Corner and had a most magnificent view from the hill onto the Epsom Downs. Tattenham Corner at the rails, was already packed with people. On the Downs there was a fair with merry-go-rounds, booths and endless bookies, the stands were already full, people were streaming in from all directions. I have never seen so many bookies offering their latest prices, and off in the distance the gentle blue hills. It looked to me like a picture by Breughal. Francis and I walked through the crowds most happily. As the stands were too expensive, even on the Downs, we secured ourselves a good position at the foot of the stands. So we could have a good view from Tattenham Corner on. The first two races didn't interest us; we sat down on the grass and ate our sandwiches and smoked. We had had no time to eat at home, as I had to work. But we enjoyed the leisure now and the hurly-burly around us. Before the main race the horses had to parade in front of the crowd and then galloped across the Down to the start. It was a big field, thirty-three horses in all! The best mover of them, so we thought, was little Tulyar, he was no more than a pony. His movements were so harmonious, round as if a circle was turning within a circle, like a spiral. We knew all the colours of the main horses. And "Off They are" in no time. Now a hush — strange that. Everyone kept their breath, even the merry-go-rounds stood still. Soon from beyond the course, near Tattenham Corner came a deep, steadily growing murmur — like an approaching wave till it reached us. Francis held his glasses fixed on the course. "Good Lord," he cried, "I see 'Bob Major' in front." My heart sank, that could not be. Racing has for us a deeper meaning — more than just the gambling. How could 'Bob Major' win a classic or even be placed in it? But there was a gap between two buses on the rails. I fixed my eyes on it — and there lo and behold — the green/chocolate hoops and chocolate cap of Tulyar's jockey, C. Smirke, flashed past in front of all the others. "But Francis, there, there is Tulyar, look, look, he is winning the race," I cried. Tulyar, our dove and angel flew like a god, hardly touching the ground! It was sheer bliss to have witnessed it.

"Tulyar, Tulyar," the crowd around shouted. That sweet little horse had won in great style — my first Derby ever! The order of the race was:

1. *Tulyar* — *C. Smirke 11.2* (but we had a better price)
2. *Gay Time* — *L. Piggot 25:1*
3. *Faubourg* — *Doyasbère 100:6*

Derby-Day at Epsom my great wish had become reality!

Soon we moved to a little shabbily furnished flat with a kitchen and room in Sinclair Gardens, near Shepherd's Bush. That house had one of the four fake columns at the front and resting on it a fake balcony, but that was ideal for Sophie. She could watch the street from there, see us coming and going, and sunbathe in it. I cleaned up the place and it was not too bad, we were left to ourselves, the rent was not too high, and the main thing no one objected to our Sophie-cat. We were mostly out working. Francis worked night-shift in the Kensington Museum — the worst of such a job is that he could not sleep during the day and his stomach got upset. In general we didn't seem able to pick up and kept constantly plodding along — but in spite of all the drudgery we didn't forget our "vespers". That kept us going.

In 1952 we had Christmas Eve on Wednesday. On Tuesday I got from Mrs. W. my present of two guineas and I hurried home so that I might do some shopping with Francis. We hadn't been able to do it before as we had no money to spare. The royalties that Francis expected from Germany hadn't come and there was now no hope for them. We had a small tree which I had been given as a Christmas gift from the other family whom I worked for every morning for two to three hours. We purchased a chicken, a bottle of wine and some other essentials with these two pounds. Then we walked home in the dusk through Holland Park at peace and content, as we thought back over other Christmases.

On Christmas Eve I worked till three. When I came home Francis looked rather mysterious and had his good suit on. I couldn't make out why. Under the tree in the corner of the kitchen he had put a bottle of white wine on a table, with a

Christmas card and round the neck of the bottle he had wrapped a piece of paper. Francis said: This is your Christmas present." But I told him to wait till the evening. I wasn't washed and dressed yet after my chores of the morning. Then the chicken had to be prepared for the oven. It surprised me a bit that Francis had got me a bottle of wine as we had bought one only the day before. And I knew he had no money.

Finally all was ready and the lights on the tree were lit. Under the tree I had put for Francis a notebook and from Sophie a lovely cat-card with ten shillings for the dog races on Boxing Day. I sang all the usual carols and then we prayed. We looked at our small presents. I didn't look especially close as I had seen already the wine. Then Francis said: "But look properly at the bottle, there is something round its neck." Then my eyes fell on the peculiar piece of tissue paper. I took it off − unwrapped it − and a most beautiful bracelet studded with small green stones fell out. I had no words and could only cry. Francis said: "The money from Germany has come." That was all too much! This money, that for various reasons, had caused us so much worry and anxiety and pain had come at the last possible moment. He had got the money-order at about lunchtime, had taken a taxi to the bank and then to the pawn shop to get his watch back, then he had bought the bottle of wine and finally the bracelet in a shop near Shepherd's Bush. He had seen it in the secondhand shop weeks ago and had had his eye on it. I can only say that as sad as our Christmas had looked in the beginning, it had turned out so beautifully, like a fairy-story come true. We were very happy, the candles had long burnt down, but the transparents with their night-lights were still glowing in the cosy, warm, kitchen. After such a hard year, all had turned out well, and Francis had at least a breathing space to finish his novel and could now give up his job.

London, January 6th, 1953:
"Just a few words only. We have got a little 'Marconi' radio which we bought on hire-purchase on Jan. 3rd. We have to pay 5/8 per week for 78 weeks. But I am in heaven with it and I don't want to stir out. It has a lovely soft sound and we can now hear music. It is nearly too much of a luxury for me. We listen now to the Rugby matches and Francis has a lot of

explaining to do about scrums, garryowens, line-outs, scores, etc. And next door is a tiny dark shop that sells Imperial Russian stout, a wonderful brew and strong on top of it.

It is very cold and today we had snow, but we have the small, warm kitchen which we heat by lighting the gas-oven and leaving the door open. I haven't been so warm for ages. We really do like this shabby Sinclair Garden flat very much, we are left in peace, and practically never see the landlady. She is happy as long as she gets her rent regularly. And now we shall have patience until Easter when we shall go to friends in the country, naturally with Sophie."

London, February 8th, 53:
"Yesterday we heard that Gollancz liked Francis' novel *The Chariot.* We were delighted with the news."

Francis's diary, February 15th, 53:
"Very cold days, but good ones in our own way. On Thursday met Martin O'Neill at White City and backed a dog he had a tip for. Though I only had eight shillings on it, and a couple for S., because I haven't much belief in these 'good' things where dogs are concerned. Martin had twenty-five pounds on it and it was beaten a neck, after leading all the way."

London, March 22nd, 1954:
"Today early in the morning Francis' wife, Iseult, died and I have just seen Francis off to Ireland. Very likely our life will change now."

Easter, April 18th, 54:
"It is a most blessed Easter inwardly and outwardly. On Good Friday we went to the Tenebrae in the Cathedral, it was a very moving service. Over Easter I decorated a black bonnet with white flowers and a black veil; the whole thing didn't cost more than fifteen shillings. I shall wear it on April 28th for our wedding in Holy Trinity, Brook Green, at 9 o'clock, with a black watered silk dress that Mary Austin gave me in Paris."

On the day of our wedding we had a small celebration and to mark our honeymoon started off for the 2,000 Guineas at Newmarket. Francis had several horses, but none obliged. I had one called 'Bride Elect' in the last race for two year old fillies

Wedding photo, April 1954, Hammersmith

Madeleine shopping in Soho Market

which I took only because of its name and it romped home to a good price. She became later a very famous broodmare. On the journey home we were delighted with the small animals we saw in the fields: two magpies (for joy!), one hare, pheasants and lots of rabbits. Very likely the ancestors of my present pet rabbit were amongst them. Everyone was tired from the outing and the cold wind, and they dozed off, only Francis could not sleep, he looked all flushed and was over-excited and over-tired as he had had worked night-shift, and was due for another one that evening. At home he just had time to change, eat something, have a drink and go off to the Geological Museum to keep guard on the precious stones there, but not before he paraded in goose-step fashion in front of the house, laughing and shouldering an imaginary gun. When I was alone I read the "Song of Solomon":

> *Come with me from Lebanon, my spouse,*
> *with me from Lebanon.*
> *Thou hast ravished my heart, my sister, my spouse;*
> *Thou hast ravished my heart with one of thine eyes,*
> *With one chain of thy neck.*

The following day was Francis' birthday. I made him stay in bed and went to work. When I came home we had a lazy afternoon, praying, preparing for supper. We went for a stroll through Holland Park. It was a lovely, mild evening, tender and green everywhere.

> *. . . lo, the winter is past,*
> *The rain is over and gone;*
> *The flowers appear on the earth;*
> *The time of the singing of birds is come*
> *And the voice of the turtle is heard in our land;*
>
> *('Song of Solomon')*

Then he went for his night-shift again.

London, Sept. 5th, 1954;
"So many good things have happened since April 28th. First I was released from my domestic chores because of our marriage. I finally got a job with Courtaulds at £6.15 per week.

Then we got this unfurnished flat in Barking Road, Canningtown, consisting of two-and-a-half rooms and a kitchen. In the kitchen there is a bath tub. I think we won't become too immersed in outward things. We shall always pray to be kept on the right path. Francis is still working in the Museum on late-shift. How nice once he enters the house and Sophie listens to his hurrying steps on the stairs. And when he opens the door she throws herself in front of him and rolls and rolls and Francis has to leave all and caress her and take her up in his arms, where she soon settles on his shoulders."

London, June 19th, 55:
"A long time has elapsed since I wrote in my diary; But I could not write as all diaries etc. were packed away in tea-chests since we moved to Barking Road. We could not unpack then, as we had no furniture to put them in. And it is only a few weeks ago since we got a military chest-of-drawers, a real beauty, into which we could pack our things. That chest cost us a cool twenty pounds, a lot of money to us, but the dealer in Portobello market said: "If you don't buy it, the next American will gladly do so." So we got it as we could not bear to see such a beautiful thing being shipped across the ocean. And then since last week we have a bookcase. So our little flat looks cosy and has even got carpets and curtains (from Courtaulds). All our furniture comes from Portobello Market. We go there every fortnight and have got some beauties. We always managed to have a pound over at the end of our purchase to christen each piece we bought with a bottle of red wine. How nice it is to do it this way, than to have everything purchased when getting married. We had moved into the unfurnished flat with only a mattress which we had bought on hire-purchase at Ponting's in South Kensington."

London, August 1955:
"Our first ever real holiday. We arrived on Tuesday, July 26th, at Dún Laoghaire and made straight for the Salthill Hotel. What an enchanting time began then. I loved it from the very beginning, especially the leisureliness of the country. On Friday, July 29th, we went to Dolores' grave (Francis' first child that died only a few months old in 1921). It is under a yew-tree, overgrown with ivy and has an oblong stone and on top of it

is a cross in relief. It is strange that when we left this long-forgotten grave, we both had the same wish to come and live in Ireland. And I thought, surely this would be the last station of our flight, otherwise we would end up in the Atlantic. And on Sunday, July 31st, we went by bus to see Francis' mother, Lily. To me it was all strange and beautiful, Francis knew every corner of the road. We had lunch in the Royal Hotel at the Lower Lake in Glendalough. There Francis met the owner, Andy, and the servants who all remembered him. We visited Iseult's grave which we found badly neglected. When we started for Francis' old home, Laragh Castle, it suddenly pelted down heavy rain. It had been very, very hot, unusual for Ireland. But Andy gave us each a raincoat. At Laragh, Lily was expecting us, sitting in her chair overlooking the long drive, holding an umbrella, but against the sun. Not a single drop had fallen here. To see Lily had also been one of my wishes. She is a lovely, gentle, old lady.

Ian, the son, showed us the house and the grounds. How sad it was when Francis pointed out all the spots and places he had so often talked about to me. There was the tree where Kay's sweet photo had been taken and which he had shown to me in Berlin's Drahtlose Dienst pub. There was the eucalyptus tree and the bamboo reeds, and then the different sheds where once Francis kept hundreds of hens. He once even got a medal for the best laying hen in Ireland! Ian drove us later to the Upper Lake, a most beautiful and holy place. It is here that St Kevin lived and prayed and said Mass in the cathedral, which is surrounded by old rainwashed tombstones. What a place for silence and meditation. Francis had this place in mind when writing in Berlin the poem 'The Upper Lake'.

Happy days, so warm with bathing and sunbathing and seeing old friends of Francis'. I enjoyed immensely Messrs Goff's Bloodstock Sales at Ballsbridge. What drama!

> *I am bid against you on my right,*
> *against you in front . . .*
> *And I am selling, gentlemen, I am selling!!!*

And bang went down the hammer and the lively yearling weighed and pranced out, already to the tune: *'Un-ter-der-La-ter-ne-'*

When we arrived home on Saturday we went first to the kennels to fetch Sophie-Heart. She was so excited and shrieked like a parrot on the way home. She grew calmer at home, but it took three days before she really was her old self again. She would follow us wherever we went. She used to hide, but when I called her, she would come running. She got thinner in the kennels and her little face with the squinting turquoise-blue eyes even sweeter.

In 1956 I changed my job and was taken on part-time at Barclays Bank. I worked fourteen days on and fourteen days off which was a glorious arrangement. We lived as if in paradise, and didn't go out as we loved our little place so much. We read together and also prayed, it was a blessed time.

London, February 3rd, 1957:
"As Francis said yesterday and it was just the right thing I needed to hear, when we had watched the first delicate green leaves of the crocuses in our backyard coming out, that these things are only so beautiful and poignant when seen against their short duration. So everything here that is beautiful must be seen against the sombre background of death to make it really beautiful. As Rilke would have it in his *"Todeserfahrung":*

> *As you went hence from this stage there*
> *shone through the gaps between the*
> *pieces of scenery through which you had gone*
> *the real greenness, the actual sunshine, the true forest.*

The fleetingness in things enhances their beauty. Without death there could not be this beauty. And that is not true only in nature, but also in art and love. "Death," as Simone Weil says, "is the centre and object of life."

My mother had died earlier that year in Poland. But I could not visit her, firstly because we didn't have the money to travel and secondly I still had Polish nationality. But one of her last words were: "I loved S (me) above all . . . I had imagined life differently." Life, especially there in Poland, was a disappointment to her, but now we were apart — irrevocably — the borders saw to it. I mention this because what S. Weil says in "Waiting for God" seems to me so appropriate.

All the circumstances of the past that have wounded our personality appear to us to be disturbances of balance which should infallibly be made up for one day or another by phenomena having a contrary effect. We live on the expectation of these compensations. The near approach of death is horrible chiefly because it forces the knowledge upon us that these compensations will never come.

(Simone Weil: 'Waiting for God',
G.P. Butnam's Sons, New York, 1951)

August, 1957:

"It is more or less settled that we are going to Ireland in September. We want to look around for a cottage. In one way we are sad when we think of leaving London, the flat is sweet, but there is too much work in offices etc. and no blade of grass around (you have to take a bus to Greenwich to see some green) and the district is very noisy. The coloured people next door run a café with slot-machine music which goes on till after twelve o'clock, and then the whole family sit down to supper at about one in the morning on the pavement outside or in the back yard.

In Ireland we went to Drogheda and from there to the races at Dundalk, where we saw Mr What, then still unknown, but who later won the Grand National at Liverpool. What a beautiful setting for the course under the Mourne mountains and how leisurely everything went on. The leisure of the people and their soft voices had struck me especially on our first visit. After the meeting on the following morning we got the local paper and there I spotted an advertisement: "Cottage, at The Reask, Dunshaughlin, Co. Meath, for sale by auction Sept. 23rd." So we made up our mind to leave Drogheda and have a look at the place. We went back to Dublin by bus, from there to Dunshaughlin on another bus and from there we took a taxi to the cottage which was four miles from the village. We looked at it and liked the setting, off the road, in the middle of rich pasture land. Francis crept into it and discovered that it had a leaking roof and no water or a toilet. But there was a well at the bottom of the garden which we later called 'Jacob's Well'. Now we had to wait for Sept. 23rd for the auction, and as we would have to be back in London, our friend Peter who was always so helpful, was willing to attend

Francis and his mother at Laragh Castle, Co. Wicklow, 1956

On Killiney beach, 1957

Reask, in 1961

the auction in Navan and bid for us. He sent us a telegram which filled us with joy:

Winner all right. Rich pasture
captured. Celebrate.
　　　　　　　　　　　　　　　　— Peter.

The cottage cost £300 and Peter paid down £75 which I think he never got back, the rest followed by cheque to "Ambrose Steen & Son", Navan. Our leisurely lifestyle now had to change. We had to work hard to get the money for the move in April and also to live on. Francis got a job in the docks as a storekeeper and I got one in Pinchin Jonson Ltd. nearby. We both could come home for a quick lunch, which was good, as my place was also near the docks. Thinking of our little cottage in the Spring of next year made the work easy. We spoke constantly of our promised land and thought of the words in the psalm:

When the Lord bringeth back the captivity of his people,
Jacob will rejoice, and Israel shall be glad.
　　　　　　　　　　　　　　　　　　　　　(Psalm 53)

Over the Easter holidays we packed books, china, etc. into tea-chests ourselves to save money, and the fact was that nothing got broken on the move. On April 16th the removal men from the British Railway would take all in a small container and we would follow on April 27th. The 'Introitus' for Easter Monday reads appropriately:

Introduxit vos Dominus
in terram fluentem lac et mel.

But before entering a new phase of our life I had to take stock of what had happened to us at the Easter of that year.
Many years ago when I was in pain and suffering I turned to the Bible, the psalms and great literature. It came quite easy and instinctively to me. I lived in those days a very intense life, having been on top of that in love and my soul was radiant in spite of all the hardships I had to endure. What I find much harder now is to keep that intensity of long ago alive and not

112

lose sight of that vision I had then. I had grasped in times of stress that there is no comfort except in God. But when I plunged into everyday life that message got blurred. I was not so foolish as to think that I could find fulfilment in earthly pleasures, but I thought that my love would stand out like a rock against all pitfalls. Gradually it dawned on me that my love is far from perfect. It is indeed very self-seeking. I had to learn that the gift of love consists mainly of fighting our own selfish, greedy, possessive ego. No wonder there were disappointments and despair galore and the heart often got broken. I am lucky that in these dark hours I was given the power to mend it time and time again. But it was not I who did the actual healing, it was a kind of grace, that pulled me out of the pit and put me on the road again, the heart a bit battered, but nonetheless intact. Rilke wrote in 'Briefe an einen jungen Dichter':

> . . . Liebhaben von Mensch zu Mensch: das ist vielleicht das Schwerste, was uns aufgegeben ist, das Ausserste, die letzte Probe und Prüfung, die Arbeit, für die alle andere Arbeit nur Vorbereitung ist. Darum können junge
> Menschen, die Anfänger in allem sind, die Liebe noch nicht: Sie müssen sie lernen . . .

(To love is difficult. To love from person to person: that is perhaps the most difficult with which we are burdened, the utmost, the last test and examination, the work, for which all other work is only a preparation.
That's why young people, who are in all beginners, aren't able to love yet, they have to learn to love.)

So I never managed to build a Jerusalem as I had hoped in the early Berlin years. And I never even got beyond the threshold of the first mansion of the 'Interior Castle'. What did I achieve then? Very little — but for me it is enough. As Francis de Sales said: "for a small dealer a small basket." What I had been able to build was a small Ark where Francis and I and my animals could take shelter from the confusion and noise and the flood of materialism of the world. And again I must quote my beloved Francis de Sales when he wrote to his friend Jeanne de Chantal: "Stay in the little boat in which I have launched you, come storm, come tempest."

EPILOGUE

The Reask, Dunshaughlin, Co. Meath; Spring 1958:
We left from Euston station on Sunday evening April 27th.
There was our old friend Peter waiting for us to say goodbye.
He had been in London for a couple of days, but could not find
us, as we had left our Barking Rd. flat and were staying with a
friend. Peter was actually in London to look for a job on the
advice of his secret fiancée. But we persuaded him to come with
us. That did not take a lot as he was a bit work-shy. The
journey and all with it and the animals (two cats by now: Lulu
and Sophie) went smoothly. I had found Lulu as a kitten in the
derelict site near St Paul's. In Dublin we had breakfast with
Maeve, Peter's friend, and then Francis and Peter left me at the
bus terminus while they went to enquire about the furniture
van. They were hardly gone when they came running back
telling me to hurry up and catch the 10 o'clock bus, as the van
was already on its way to the cottage. In Dunshaughlin we got
some provisions, hired a taxi and then in a fine drizzle we drove
like a king and queen to our Promised Land. Near the cottage
we saw the postman enquiring from somebody on the road
about something. He was looking for a Mr Francis Stuart!
They had never heard of him in these parts. And he really had
our first post which were cards for Francis' birthday on April
29th. I had told all our friends in London to shower us with
post and make a splash. And a few yards from us drove the
British Railway van, quite steady, although swaying a bit — it
was a touching sight. We both arrived together at the gate of
the cottage. That was timing, from London to The Reask! This
Monday was our wedding anniversary, so we had a lot to
celebrate! But we had the necessary red wine bottles with us.

And there in my joy and gratitude I knew we had come full-circle. I knew in my heart that the star from Munich times now would stand steadfast over our new lovely cottage. Our flight and wandering had come to an end;

> *They that sow in tears shall reap in joy.*
> *He that goeth forth and weepeth, bearing precious seed,*
> *Shall doubtless come again with rejoicing, bringing his*
> *   sheaves with him.*
> *The Lord hath done great things for them.*

(Psalm 126)

Francis and Madeleine Stuart, Dublin, 1984
(Photo: Philip Casey, Raven Arts)